MW01614828

BREAKING
THE
STUPID

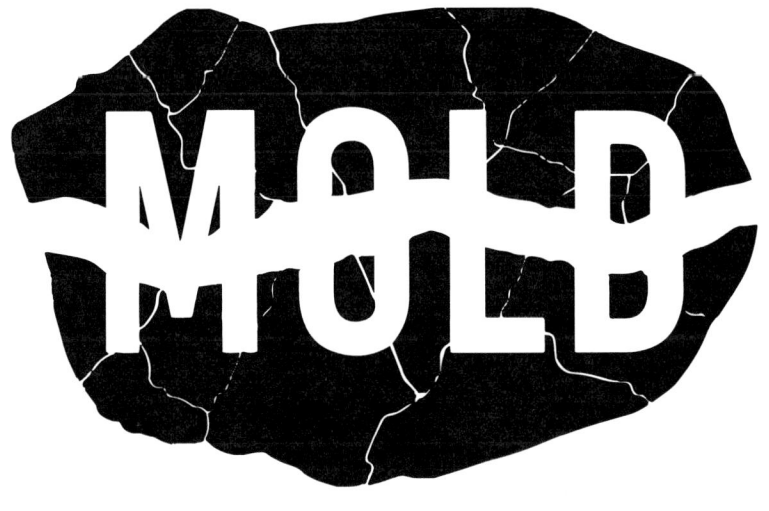

TANIA KOLAR

BREAKING
THE
STUPID
MOLD

Overcoming Self-Sabotage And Limiting Beliefs,
So You Can Live **An Extraordinary Life**

Authenticity Speaks
PUBLISHING

COPYRIGHT © 2019 BY TANIA KOLAR

For more information, address: tania@taniakolar.com

The author of this book does not dispense medical advice nor prescribe the use of any technique as a form of treatment for physical or mental problems without the advice of a physician or health care professional either directly or indirectly. The intent of the author is only to offer information of a general nature to help you in your quest for spiritual, emotional and physical wellbeing. In the event you use any of the information in this book for yourself, the author and the publisher assume no responsibility for your actions.

FIRST EDITION

Cover design by Maria Stoian

ISBN: 978-1-9990510-0-6

Published By Authenticity Speaks Publishing

www.taniakolar.com

DEDICATION

This book is dedicated with boundless love to my nieces and nephew, Alexandra (Alex) Boyd, Stephen Boyd, Sarah Boyd, and Emma Boyd. Through the inevitable cycle of life's ups and downs, may you always remember to live the extraordinary life you were meant to live and never doubt for a moment how deeply cherished, loved and extraordinary you are.

CONTENTS

ACKNOWLEDGEMENTS

With deep gratitude and heartfelt thanks to Garett Gratton for your unshakeable belief and support in me, I love you.

To my dear friend Pat DeVellis (Big Pat) for graciously lending an ear and providing constructive criticism and indispensable feedback as I read and reread chapter after chapter aloud to you. Your patience and friendship is a gift.

To Jay Chagnon for being a radiant light. Thank you for encouraging me to share my voice and reminding me to recognize and acknowledge my strengths and talents. Then gently nudging me forward when I wavered.

To Jacqui Stafford, for countless conversations abounding with substance and heart and for standing by me and believing in me even when others didn't. I look forward to our customary get-togethers (never long enough) and can't wait for the next one.

Special thanks to Basia Palmer for being with me every step of the way on this emotional journey. Your contribution and support were invaluable throughout this process. Your notes of encouragement were uplifting and kept me motivated and inspired. Thank you for being my biggest fan.

To Diane Kolar for helping me tweak the book cover design to match my vision, even though you had your hands full with your precious sons, Benjamin and baby William and had no free time to spare.

To Ann Boyd, Henry Kolar, Nancy Kekic, Alexandra Boyd (Alex), Stephen Boyd, Sarah Boyd, Emma Boyd, Patricia DeVellis (Little Pat), Piera Cornelio and the rest of my family and friends for your understanding and support throughout this journey and for tolerating my absence as I carved out time to realize a dream and write this book. I am eternally grateful for each of you.

And to all the inspirational thought leaders who have gone before me that imparted wisdom and knowledge through their teachings and helped me become the person who I am today. I am forever in your debt.

A LETTER TO THE READER

In 2006, I was the victim of a violent encounter with a stranger. This ordeal abruptly interrupted my life, and the carefully controlled world I had come to know began to unravel swiftly. I didn't know it at the time, but out of suffering would come one of my greatest rewards, and my life would forever be altered.

My world was shaken by this trauma, and as a result, I experienced deep emotional pain and PTSD. I was left broken and afraid and felt like I was losing control. I did my best to hide my pain and portray that I was fine. You see, from the outside looking in, I was the person who had it all together. I was the person that took care of everyone else when they needed support or someone to be there. I was there for others but I didn't even have it within me to know how to let others support or take care of me, so I didn't let them. What no one knew, was that behind my smile I didn't know if or how I was going to recover. One thing I did know for sure, is that I refused to let a stranger control my life, so I pushed through the pain and forged ahead with a fixed determination trying to make sense of what happened.

I began a journey of deep introspection and self-discovery which unexpectedly revealed to me that I never really had the control I thought I had and that there was something else dictating my decisions, behaviors, and controlling every aspect of my life. I discovered I was programmed by my past to shrink from my potential. I had a lifetime's worth of limiting beliefs that were sabotaging my life. I was being controlled by what I call a "mold" a false identity filled with limiting beliefs. I wasn't willing to let a stranger control my life, and yet somehow I had inadvertently let this mold control my entire existence.

I discovered how to break through my limiting beliefs, self-doubt, and self-sabotage and take back control of my life. I feel called to share my story so that you can identify and break through your limitations and subconscious behaviors that prevent you from being the best version of yourself.

I want you to know that when life knocks you down so hard that it's difficult to breathe that you have the strength within you to stand back up even though you are afraid, even though you can't see ahead and you don't know how you're going to get through your most difficult challenges. I want you to stand up as the extraordinary person you are and move forward by putting one foot in front of the other and rise to your best self. For all the times you've hidden your pain, sadness grief or vulnerability or pretended to be someone you're not, I want you to know that you are enough and to find your voice, speak your truth and let your inner light shine to illuminate the darkness.

Find the purpose in your pain, trauma, loss, sadness, grief, heartbreak, despair, and suffering. When you have a willingness to pick yourself up despite your pain, sadness, grief, tears, fears, and challenges you create an opening for something better to enter your life and the next steps to take will naturally unfold for you. Your path will be lit, and you will be guided to regain the sense of self you lost.

In sharing my experience and my truth, I wish to inspire and empower you to move beyond limitation, doubt, and challenges, piece the lost parts of yourself back together and find your wholeness and claim the life of greatness that was destined for you. You are unique and have special gifts that no one else has. There is no one else on the planet like you. I want you to dare to be you and share your authentic self with the world because you have so much more to offer than you could ever imagine.

Be the extraordinary person you are and live the extraordinary life you were meant to live!

With love and gratitude,

Tania

1

THE INVISIBLE DICTATOR
BURIED IN YOUR SUBCONSCIOUS

"In the darkest moments come the most illuminate teachings."
– Tania Kolar

Your greatest challenges in life can be your greatest rewards if you open your eyes wide enough and long enough to detect them. Several years ago, I was challenged to open my eyes long and wide which led to my deepest life inquiry and greatest lesson. I was attacked, beaten, strangled and sexually assaulted by a stranger in an underground parking lot. The attack was unusually violent for a stranger against another stranger, so the police believed someone was hired to kill me. I began to question everything. Why did this happen? How could this happen to me? What did I do to deserve this? I questioned not only why it happened but also my reaction to it. Why was I downplaying the severity of what happened? Why was I pretending I was fine when I was an emotional wreck? Why wasn't I able to share what I was going through?

During my struggle to find the answers, the decay of my past was revealed to me. I finally understood what was subconsciously driving all my decisions. There was something deep below the surface of my thoughts that was controlling my behavior. I discovered what I call a "mold" that was dictating my life from the sidelines. I call it a mold because it was shaped and formed like soft, malleable clay, set, hardened and solidified over time, becoming fixed and immoveable until broken. Thus creating a matrix of a mold, a false identity that would become a reality. This mold was chock full of limiting beliefs and was destroying my potential.

Every one of us, including you, has a mold, a false self that runs our lives. This stupid mold has been sabotaging us. As a result, we have become our own worst critics. We incessantly beat ourselves up for the perceived mistakes we've made, the injustices we've created or even the missed opportunities that we carelessly let slip by. We continue to say terrible things to ourselves because of old beliefs. Don't let your past define you and limit your future happiness. You are not your past. You are far greater than the sum of your past. I learned how to break from the clutches of my mold and turned a traumatic ordeal into a profound lesson. In this book, I will show you how to break free from the constraints of your mold and turn your greatest challenges into your greatest rewards.

I have researched and studied personal development for over twenty-five years. I have read hundreds of books, attended workshops and seminars and listened to podcasts, taking in the works of inspirational thought leaders, continually trying to find something. I had an innate sense that there was more to the life I was living and that somehow I was the one standing in the way and preventing it. This fueled my pursuit to search for something greater. I have amalgamated my knowledge of self-development and personal experience and discovered how to break through the limiting beliefs of my past, and I will teach you how to do the same.

How many times do you repeat the same patterns in life? Do you feel that no matter what you do you always get the same outcomes? Do you experience the same problems, the same struggles, and the same obstacles? Do you have the same arguments, attract the same kind of partner or keep going back to the people or things that end up hurting you? Well, you are definitely not alone. We all have a tendency to repeat patterns that lead us down a familiar pathway the road to inferiority. Why are we on this inferior pathway? We are driven by this matrix of a mold that reinforces and hails our limitations. This limiting mold keeps us stuck on repeat, and it prevents us from living our best life. A mold is created from the repetition of negative thoughts, habits, patterns, and beliefs. It starts out formless and empty and is shaped by whatever we choose to put into it.

In the first stages of development, a mold can take on any form. However, over time, with a barrage of the same thoughts over and over, we draw in more of the same leaving little room for that which is unfamiliar. Life experiences, our thoughts, memories, prejudices, insecurities and negative beliefs all accumulate. A mold can be comprised of both negative and positive attributes working either for you or against you. Unfortunately, for most people the negative mold dominates. It works against you, and you are stuck living a second-rate life.

As a mold gets larger it becomes partial to what is already there and like a magnet, draws in more of what dominates and begins to repel the opposite. We act and react based on what the mold is saying. Hence we continue to play out familiar and predictable patterns. This mold is not real, it's created, and it's the foundation for all our decisions. It's the invisible dictator buried in your subconscious controlling every aspect of your life and sabotaging your future. A mold is a false identity that causes you to fall short of your full potential and has you living an ordinary and mundane existence. Your true identity is buried beneath your mold in the space that existed before you created it. This space is where all potentiality exists, and you can create an extraordinary life from it. A life you thought was never possible for you.

My wish for you dear reader is to smash through the mold that restricts you from living your best life.

I will guide you through easy and practical techniques to take back control of the extraordinary life you were born to live. You're meant to live the life that awakens your passions and ignites your soul. A life that is unencumbered by self-sabotage or limiting beliefs. All experiences, especially the difficult ones, have contributed to your beliefs and the creation of a false self. When you discover and break the mold that erroneously defines you, you will inch closer to your best self and transform your life. In *The Way of The Peaceful Warrior*, Dan Millman says, "Mediocrity is for the fence sitters of the world." I urge you to jump off the fence and release the inherent greatness that is you. Jump... you've got this!

2

DETOUR OFF THE ROAD TO INFERIORITY

"The surrender of life is nothing to sinking down into acknowledgment of inferiority."
– John C. Calhoun

I magine traveling down a vast never-ending highway with unlimited on/off ramps and connector roads. This highway represents your journey in life. There are endless possible routes you can take. You can get to any destination you want on this highway. For the most part, it's smooth sailing, and you enjoy the ride until suddenly, you hit a roadblock that prevents you from going any further. A roadblock represents any of life's challenges. Some roadblocks are minor while others are catastrophic. What do you do when you encounter roadblocks? Most likely, you will decide to follow the detour, take an alternate route or turn around and go back the same way you came. When you hit the first roadblock, you are free to choose how to react because you have no preconceived notions of what to expect. You continue to coast along the roadway to your next destination and eventually, bam, you hit another roadblock. Now, this is when you remember the first block. Your memory of the first block creates all kinds of beliefs around it, and you react according to those initial beliefs.

Your behavior at any subsequent roadblocks is greatly influenced by how you handled the first one and the second one and so on. You have now created a pattern and are conditioned to favor that behavior. If you were slightly annoyed at the first block, on subsequent blocks, you would keep adding to that annoyance. So, you go from being slightly irritated to really angry after you've hit more and more blocks. Since you have been fueling your mold after every life challenge, your reaction is bigger and disproportionate to the current situation. Therefore, even when you hit a minor block, you act from a place of great anger.

Do you ever notice when you are having an argument with your significant other, the disagreement seems to expand beyond what you were initially arguing about? You are arguing from past arguments that are resurfacing and not the current argument. Many times you can't even remember what you were arguing about, but you are so consumed by anger you can't let it go. Your mold is controlling your behavior during the argument. It's pulling up past beliefs, and now you are reacting from what your mold is saying and not the actual argument.

The journey on the road to inferiority is full of limitations. Many you have created for yourself, and others are destined by fate or karma. No matter the cause, it is always in your control to either accept or break from limitations. When you've hit a lot of roadblocks, eventually you learn to avoid the routes that have blocks. Avoiding such routes, because you've hit roadblocks there before, is akin to avoiding life. When bad things happen, you ignore it and hope it will disappear. The problem is, you get so used to ignoring your life that eventually you stop taking chances and ignore your own desires and you run the risk of forgetting what your desires even were. You are now officially stuck driving down the road of inferiority getting unexceptional results. Let's take a look at a few ways you may be driving down this highway and limiting your potential.

There's the procrastinator type personality. The procrastinator is afraid to take action and wants to avoid stress. They know they should have gotten off several exits ago but couldn't commit to a decision. So, instead, they pass all the exits and continue driving down the road to inferiority, missing out on life's opportunities. Then there's the workaholic who's been moving too fast and not appreciating the journey along the way. This can be when you don't spend enough time with your partner, kids or loved ones. You have the best intentions, but your priorities are not in the right place. You're so busy taking every connecting roadway that you miss the joy of the ride. Or there's the reckless personality. This is a person who makes careless or dangerous choices with little or no regard to the consequences of their actions or puts others at risk also. Then there's the avoider who pretends everything is okay when they know their life is a complete mess. For example, their spouse told them they were unhappy in the marriage and suggested they both go to marriage counseling. They refused to accept there was a problem with the relationship and declined the opportunity to fix the marriage. Then down the road, they found out their spouse had been having an affair, and now wants a divorce.

Then you have the victim. When they encounter roadblocks, they feel victimized. If things don't turn out the way they wanted, they believe someone else is at fault. In a head-on collision, a victim will say things like "It's not my fault, it's not fair, I didn't cause this; this can't be happening to me, someone else needs to fix this." Or they say, "I'll never get through this." A head-on collision represents any significant challenge. You cannot be empowered to take action and be a victim at the same time. If you take responsibility for what has happened in your life, you can find the benefit in your suffering, and you will no longer feel victimized.

Next, you have the person who is never satisfied, and always looking for a better or faster route or change their destination when they are on their way to somewhere else. This can be likened to someone who jumps from relationship to relationship because they are never satisfied with their current situation and are always searching for something better. Then there's the person who is always overworked and running on empty. They feel drained, overwhelmed and won't ask for help. This is a person that has to do everything themselves and has trouble delegating because they can't admit they need help.

There are many different types of drivers on the road to inferiority. Some of them overlap, and you can be several types at any given time. You can take charge of the wheel as you steer your vehicle down the highway and stop driving on autopilot. Be the kind of driver you want to be, not the one chosen by default through bad conditioning (your mold) and choose the life you want to live. Unbeknownst to you, you've had a passenger with you for the entire ride. This passenger is your mold. It's been making every decision for you. It's guided you on which exits and roads to take or avoid. The longer you've been driving on the road to inferiority the stronger the pull to keep you on it.

Once you realize you've been steered in the wrong direction, you can kick your unwelcome passenger off at the next exit. You are then free to make your own decisions and get to wherever you want to go by relying on your internal sense of direction. Use your internal compass to guide you. It's your built-in guidance system, your intuition. If you use it, it will never steer you wrong.

The problem is most people have their internal compass turned off. This is when you ignore your instinct and any signs the Universe is sending you. Your internal compass knows how to navigate around the roadblocks which eventually lead to your final destination. Your internal compass knows how to get there. You can't hear the guidance because of the overpowering mold voice that dictates your direction. Ignoring your intuition is like driving blindfolded.

You already have all the answers you need within you. Your internal compass is always ready to direct you to the best routes based on your current position, that is, wherever you are in any given moment of your life, but you must use the compass in order to benefit from its' guidance. Turn on your internal compass to find the best routes to take and learn how to navigate the roadblocks/ life challenge's in the best possible way.

Your mold is now loaded with experiences as you drive down the road of inferiority. Your road trip has determined the quality of your life in all areas. If you are not living your dream life, you must break your mold and move in the direction of your best life. Strive to be the driver who hits all the green lights, and manages to avoid traffic jams. When you are driving on the right path, you are no longer resigned to the choices being made for you by limiting beliefs. You catch all the green lights, and you move along with ease. When a roadblock pops up, you understand it's only temporary. You make peace with each roadblock and take the necessary actions to continue down the highway. You accomplish your goals or at least have a good idea of how to get there.

When you break from the mold that has been driving all your decisions you travel down the highway knowing that you can choose to take any exit you wish. Even when you have a destination in mind you know, you can easily adjust your course if it feels right. You learn to trust and follow your instinct. When you spot a signpost in the distance, that reads "The Road to Greatness, next exit" without hesitation, you click on your indicator light and take the next exit.

Every roadblock/life challenge you've encountered has provided you with the lessons needed to steer you to your best self. When you are on the road to greatness the road to inferiority can no longer exist for you. Take that final detour from living a mediocre life and drive straight down the road to greatness where unlimited possibility is already yours. It's there waiting for you, you just need to break through limiting beliefs to catch up to it. We have mistakenly come to believe our patterns define who we truly are. They keep us safely sheltered in comfort zones where we avoid pain and risk at all costs. We subconsciously protect ourselves which does nothing but inhibits living to our fullest potential. Limiting our potential leads directly down the road to inferiority. As you head down the road of inferiority, you are happy with the status quo because it feels safe and familiar. You coast along, not taking chances because you've convinced yourself things don't feel so bad.

The problem is, in the long term, things don't feel so good either because you've put a cap on your happiness. The Universe is infinitely abundant. There are no limits. The only limits are the ones you created for yourself. You stay in the slow lane and never bother to change lanes because it feels comfortable. This creates inaction. This is like staying in a loveless relationship because, at this moment, it feels safer and more comfortable than being alone. Although it may feel good in the short term, over time, it is stifling. Action is necessary to progress in life. If there is no progress, there is no growth. If there is no growth, there are no results. When you don't take action because you want to avoid the discomfort, it kills results and your happiness. You can never reach your full potential or be the person you were born to be by always playing it safe or taking the easy route.

Like the ups and downs of life, every red light is guaranteed to turn green at some point. You will get the green light, the go-ahead in your life. Your greatest life lessons are in the roadblocks you encounter along your pathway. Examine the roadblocks and signs along the way. You have a big bold, beautiful life waiting for you. Edge past your comfort zone bit by bit and fight through the fear to reach it. In this book, I will teach you how to break free from your stupid mold, detour off the road of inferiority to the road of greatness and get the results you want in all areas of your life. Remember, that greatness is your birthright, and every experience is an opportunity to help get you there. Enjoy the journey to your best self, roadblocks and all.

3

SYMPTOMS OF SELF-SABOTAGE
AND RESULTING BEHAVIORS

*"Self-sabotage is like a game of mental tug-of-war. It is the conscious
mind versus the subconscious mind where the subconscious mind always
eventually wins."*
— *Bo Bennett*

A m old is deeply buried within your subconscious. It operates in the background manipulating and controlling your thoughts and ultimately sabotaging your success. Sabotage can show up in a number of unsuspecting ways, but always negatively impacting your life. Here are a few symptoms of sabotage affecting your life.

- You play small for fear of how others will react if you are successful.
- You quit just when you are close to the finish line

because you believe you don't deserve to win.

- You deliberately say something foolish, so others believe you are less intelligent than you are.
- You avoid sharing your opinion because you're afraid to be judged.
- You hide your vulnerability because you believe crying is a weakness.
- You act submissive in relationships because you're afraid to stand up for yourself.
- You avoid making decisions because you can't handle being wrong
- You continue to attract men who are controlling or women who emasculate you.

These are all symptoms of sabotage showing up in your life because of your controlling mold. So, how do you know if you have a mold that's sabotaging your life? If you are experiencing any of the following resulting behaviors or feelings on a frequent and recurring basis your stupid mold is the guilty culprit:

- procrastination/pay bills late/being late for everything
- jealousy/envy
- insecurity/feeling inadequate/unworthiness
- obsessive/compulsive/overspending
- attraction to losers
- avoid relationships, intimacy or commitment
- exaggerate/overdramatize things
- being a people pleaser/agree with others even

though you disagree
- helpless/a need to be rescued/playing the victim
- defiance/rebellion
- an overwhelming sadness/anger
- controlling or manipulative/being a bully
- needing to be in a relationship/co-dependent
- needing to do everything yourself/perfectionism
- settling for less than you know you deserve/staying in an unfulfilling relationship
- complain even when things are going well
- needing attention/manifest illness to get attention
- needing validation/needing approval/needing to prove yourself
- never apologize/always apologize
- distrusting/compulsive lying

You have come to believe what you can or cannot become or achieve because of what has been deeply imprinted into your subconscious and buried in your mold. In many instances, you have picked up that negative conditioning during your childhood simply by observing and mimicking behavior from parents, siblings or caregivers or anyone you spend a lot of time with. You fall prey to subtle indoctrination by inheriting the limitations of those around you. When you are subjected to other's insecurities on a regular basis, you run the risk of adopting their behaviors and beliefs and adding them to your mold.

If you are repeatedly made to feel you are worthless, useless, no good, a loser or that you will never amount to anything, eventually you believe it. The roles people play reinforcing this in our lives creates a strong belief you are less than and you will create a reality that coincides with that belief. These people are our role models, we look up to them, trust them, and believe them. This is not who you truly are at your core. You have created a false identity, and you begin to live from an inauthentic place.

You act as others see you instead of living from your core truth. For example, if others believe you are timid and shy and have convinced you of the same, you will avoid acting expressive and powerful even though you possess the skills and are fully capable of being this way. Another example is adopting a certain behavior in order to receive the love or approval you crave. As a young girl, you may have behaved masculine in order to receive love from a father or father figure who valued strength or assertiveness, favored your brother or punished you for being feminine. If you are repressing authentic behaviors and replacing them with behaviors others expect from you, you must challenge your beliefs, or you will become who they believe you are.

You can become so disassociated from who you truly are you may not even recognize yourself. Little by little your true identity is hidden away. You believe you are a bad person or not good enough, or a whole list of descriptors based on limiting beliefs. You must find your truth, and stop believing in the lies you have told yourself based on what others have persuaded you to believe. It's a total absurdity! On a subconscious level, you've turned against yourself and become your own worst enemy. The tougher you are on yourself, the bigger the gap you create for others to love and support you fully.

No one has the power to choose your beliefs or how you feel unless you give up your power to them. It's within your power to change your thoughts and create a new way of thinking that will challenge your entire belief system. You can stop the sabotage that shows up and destroys any progress, by rewiring your conditioned programming. You can do this by creating what is known as a new neural pathway. To create a new neural pathway you must first identify negative thought patterns, next change them into positive thought patterns, and then train your brain to reinforce the new positive thoughts through repetition. As you use positive thought patterns, you are rewiring your conditioned negative programming and creating space for something new. You will learn a new way of being and create new experiences. Something better will appear when you take a departure from previous sabotaging thought patterns. Creating a new neural pathway is like finding a shorter and faster route to your desired destination. It will become infinitely easier to reach your dreams, goals and become a better you.

It is important to remember who you are and reconnect with source energy. Source energy is pure, positive, high vibrational energy/frequency. When you are attuned to this universal source energy, your struggles seem to disappear, and life becomes effortless. You can create anything and everything you desire with unexplained ease and knowingness. Suddenly, the right people will come into your life to assist you. Previous doubt is replaced by a sense of knowing that you will achieve that which you set out to accomplish. You believe in yourself and no longer second guess your decisions or doubt your success.

Silence the inner critic that constantly shoots you down and sabotages your success. Get present to your life and challenge your thoughts and behaviors. When you live with mindful awareness in the now your future defaults to one of authenticity. If you haven't been living authentically, or feel unsatisfied with your life, this is your chance to change your story and create the future you want. It's never too late to rewrite your story and create the life you desire.

If you feel love was withheld from you, change your story by giving yourself what you needed most but didn't receive. Revisit that time in your mind and see all the characters in your story as vulnerable and impressionable children. Imagine they are all six years old. When you turn an adult into a six-year-old, they are no longer frightening, intimidating or controlling and they lose their power over you. Try to find compassion for the six-year-old that didn't know any better at the time.

We are all doing the best we can at any given moment. Change the scenarios and give yourself what you needed most but didn't get to feel or experience. We are all worthy of receiving. It is time for you to recognize your worthiness. I want you to take a moment now to honor your worthiness. Really feel it and let it soak in and acknowledge and appreciate your own worth. How do you feel? What do you need to feel better? Do you need to be consoled, comforted, loved, protected or validated? Do you want to feel needed? You may want to feel safe and loved because you felt you weren't worth receiving that kind of attention.

In addition, you may feel as if you don't know how to handle receiving the attention. You may be so used to protecting everyone else and worrying about their feelings that your own feelings become unimportant and nearly non-existent. The story that you tell yourself and believe is a relentless falsehood that manifests in many different forms and appears in all areas even when you least expect it. Like for me when one of the constables working on my case came to my door. She told me they made a huge mistake. What I heard was that I was not important. After being violently attacked and assaulted, I still believed I was unworthy of help. I couldn't comprehend that an entire police unit had devoted countless manpower hours to my case. I thought, surely there was someone more important.

Thanks to my limiting beliefs, the crossed circuits in my conditioned brain went into overdrive. I was processing information from my mold and in a matter of seconds what I heard was "it was a mistake helping you. You are not good enough to be helped. You don't deserve all this attention. There is someone else more deserving of police support. You are not important. It is a waste of time helping you. You are stealing time away from others who are more important." This was the garbage running through my head. I felt sick to my stomach and had to catch my breath and ask the police officer to repeat what she said. Then, I understood what she really said, without inserting my beliefs. She didn't say they made a mistake helping me, but rather they made a mistake distributing information.

What she was trying to explain was they accidentally mixed up documents intended for police information, with a public flyer asking for the public's assistance in finding the attacker. The flyer was handed out to every unit in the townhouse complex across from where I lived. It contained personal information including my name, address, and details of the attack. A woman who received one of the flyers, called the police department to say she believed the victim would not appreciate having her name and info shared with the public. She was right. I grew up in that townhouse complex and was mortified that people would know what happened.

However, I was used to playing the martyr, so I wasn't supposed to be angry or upset. So, instead of letting on I was upset, I told the officer I was going to look for the positive and maybe this happened for a reason. Perhaps, somehow it would lead to finding my attacker. I wondered if he lived in the townhouse complex. Or if perhaps, someone would be able to identify him. Finding the positive in any circumstance is beneficial. However, it is important to express your feelings and be honest with yourself. Don't pretend to be positive to avoid your feelings. Your denial about your feelings may be masquerading as positivity.

I was told by the chief of police that my case ranked as one of the worst top five cases he had seen in his twenty-some-odd year career. I was shaken by his words but still didn't feel worthy of the help. I began to search for the reason why I reacted this way. Slowly, I started to become aware of the destructive thoughts and negative patterns that high-jacked my thinking. I realized my past beliefs were controlling my present reactions, not only in this situation but in all areas of my life. When I recounted my conversation with the constable I concluded, I was reacting to a lifetime of other accumulated beliefs. I couldn't clearly hear what she was saying because I subconsciously added layers of thoughts from past programming to her words. Her words were compounded at that moment by a rush of adverse thoughts. I scrutinized my thoughts and began to separate the old from the new. I felt as if I was teetering on the edge of a breakthrough or total breakdown.

4

MESSAGES FROM
THE UNIVERSE

*"When we're consciously aware, we receive the messages the Universe
sends to answer us through intuition that could be easily missed if we
weren't living in the moment. These messages will guide us to our true
path."*
– Nanette Mathews

The Universe is both a constant source and a reliable
provider of life lessons. As reliable as the cycles of
day and night, you can be assured life lessons will
emerge to challenge you, provide opportunities for growth,
and help guide you on your life path. Life lessons appear as a
gentle or not so gentle nudge from the Universe to help you
uncover your authentic self. This is the self that is hidden by
your mold that you can uncover. When you live authentically
and live your truth, your soul is alive and ignited with a
genuine passion for life. You are here, on this planet to be
your authentic self. Your true identity is unencumbered by

negative thoughts, patterns, habits, and beliefs. This is the self you want to share with the world.

You may not recognize life lessons or understand the intended message at first, however, if you don't get the lesson on the first attempt, in all likelihood, it will keep coming back around until you understand and can embrace what the lesson is offering to teach you. Life lessons manifest themselves in many different ways. Recurring dreams, memories, and words are all sources of invaluable life lessons. They provide great insight into what steps to take to get from where you are to where you want to be.

Let's take a look at recurring dreams. Your mind is always working, even during sleep. While you are sleeping your mind is working out the problems you had earlier in the day. Your dreams can provide the missing link, that one piece of information or thing needed to provide the solution to the problem you're struggling with. When you wake up, try and remember any dreams you had. You will be more inclined to find the solution that is there for you if it is still fresh in your subconscious mind. You may be surprised to discover the solution to the problem you couldn't sort out the day before.

Another source of a divine message is reading or hearing a recurring word or song that plays over and over in your mind for no apparent reason. If you hear a song repeatedly in your mind, it's a good idea to look up the song's lyrics. Study the lyrics until you find the link and what it personally means to you. A message may be contained in one word, a few lines of the lyrics, the chorus or the song title itself and may recur within one day, over the course of a few days or several weeks. If you look long enough and hard enough, you will discover the meaning to these messages. It may be a signal from the Universe that you're on the right or perhaps the wrong path. For example, if you're going through a difficult relationship or personal challenge and the song, "I Will Survive", is playing on the car radio, and when you switch to the next station, it's playing again, and later that same day when you're out shopping you hear it playing in the background. I'd say that's a divine message, to let you know you will get through this challenging time. If you are experiencing financial hardship and several times throughout the week you catch yourself singing, "We're in the Money"! Which is a song you're unlikely to sing, and you have no idea why you are singing it, you can be sure it's a sign your financial situation will improve. If you were offered a dream job, on the condition you relocate to a different city and you don't know whether or not you should accept the offer, because the thought of moving is daunting and every time you contemplate what you should do, the song "New York, New York" plays in your mind or you hear the song "Leaving on a Jet Plane" for several days in a row, this is a divine message from the Universe that you should not be overwhelmed by the thought of moving, and take the job.

Recurring memories also provide meaningful life lessons. A recurring memory may seem insignificant at the moment, in which case it's easy to dismiss it as having no value. However, if the memory keeps returning to you, there is definitely something there for you to discover. You may have to dig deep to decipher what the message and the meaning is, but it is there and can provide valuable insight. The key is to recognize any patterns that can help you understand why the memory has resurfaced. Recurring memories always have a reason for why they return. Go back in time to the moment. Who was there? What were you doing? What were you feeling? Or, what feelings were you repressing? Once you discover the lesson within, the memory will no longer repeat itself.

I had a memory that kept popping up. Initially, I thought nothing of it. However, it came to mind so many times, I intuitively knew there was a reason this particular memory kept cropping up. There was something I hadn't discovered yet, and I went to work to figure it out. The memory was from my childhood. I was about five years old. One afternoon, I was playing on the front steps of the old church beside our home. I was skipping, and I accidentally missed a step, I tripped and fell down the concrete steps. Both of my knees were scraped and bleeding. I was crying, and tears were streaming down my face.

I ran as fast as I could bursting into my father's shop to get help. He stopped talking to his customer, took one look at me, standing there hurt, bruised, scraped, my knees bleeding, and my tears streaming down my face, and all he did was call me a "stupid kid" and told me to, "get lost!" I was completely mortified. I ran upstairs to the apartment we lived in above my father's shop. I sat alone in my bedroom, with the curtains drawn, in the dark, feeling totally rejected. I wished I had never fallen down the steps. I wished I never cried, and I wished I never ran into my father's shop. The words "stupid kid" kept running through my mind. It was in that moment I locked in a limiting belief. I truly believed I was stupid for falling down the stairs. I was ashamed of my tears and ashamed of myself for being stupid. From that moment on, I created a false belief from the negative thoughts running through my head. And so became my on-going story; I was just a stupid kid. When I accidentally slammed my finger in the car door, I tried not to cry. I wasn't always successful at holding back the tears, but I was determined to give it my best shot. I believed that if I cried that would show everybody, I was stupid so I decided not to cry.

The belief that I was stupid factored into many other scenarios. Shortly after, the experience I had in my father's shop, I can remember carrying a stack of my parent's Elvis and Sinatra vinyl records under my arm. I had more records than I could carry in my small arms, so the records came sliding out of the sleeves and landed on my big toe. It hurt, and I wanted to cry, but I wouldn't let myself. I linked crying and being vulnerable to being weak and stupid, so I held back my tears. By the end of the day, my toe turned purple. I did my best to ignore the pain. Later that night my mother noticed my toe. She made me a soothing foot bath and tended to my sore toe. She wanted to know why I didn't tell her earlier. The truth was, I believed I was "stupid" for dropping the records, and I wanted to keep my secret from her and everyone else. So, I hid my injury and suppressed my feelings to avoid revealing the truth.

While I was growing up whenever I made a mistake

be it big or small, the word "stupid" was always running through my head something like "Oh Tania, you're so stupid, you're such a stupid kid, how could you be so stupid!" For years, I was haunted by the words my father said to me on the day I burst into his shop. If my dad were alone, I believe he would have comforted me. He was so concerned about being judged by the customer that he sent me away without consoling me. My dad was acting from a place of past conditioning. He was not a cruel man. He was gentle, loving and hardworking. What I have come to realize is that my father had his own insecurities. My dad linked his identity to his work. He felt important in being an electrician. When I interrupted him by running into his shop, I challenged his identity and brought out his insecurities. He felt small and inadequate and not as successful as he was trying to portray, so, at that moment, he rejected me to maintain his identity and avoid feeling unworthy.

My father's words and the rejection I felt, created the beginnings of a mold which would control my life from that point on. Like a magnet, I attracted more scenarios to make me feel stupid and kept adding them to the mold I created. I subconsciously ignored or filtered any evidence contrary to the limiting belief I was stupid. I spent decades believing I was still just a stupid kid who shouldn't express her feelings. Throughout the years, I unwittingly perpetuated this belief. Subconsciously, I made it my mission to prove I was a "stupid kid." For many years, I portrayed myself as being less intelligent than I was. I would avoid sharing things I knew about and shunned being part of some conversations. And on occasion, I would say or do something deliberately to make me look unintelligent. When others told me how smart I was, I dismissed their comments and steadfastly held on to the belief I was stupid.

Stupid is a false perception I created from the meaning I gave to my father's words. Showing your vulnerability and crying or shedding a few tears because you're hurt has nothing to do with being stupid. The little girl who tumbled down the church steps was never stupid, and neither are you for that matter. Let your inner child have a good cry. You only have one chance to live this life. Don't hold yourself back or waste precious time living false beliefs. Take back control of your life and destroy your mold filled with false beliefs so you can live your life authentically and with passion.

A great way for you to discover your false beliefs is to pay close attention to how you negatively address yourself, particularly when you've done something wrong. What do you say to yourself when you've done something wrong or failed at something? Do you tell yourself you are stupid, an idiot or a fool? Do you call yourself a loser, ugly, useless, or lazy? Take note of what you think when you accidentally bump into a doorway, when you break a glass, when you say the wrong thing, pay the same bill twice or forget an appointment. Your thoughts, in these moments, are beliefs from inside your created mold. Your mold is working very hard to make your thoughts and beliefs a reality. What you have created in your mold is what you will act out or portray. Remember though, this is a false identity and is deceiving.

From the outside, you may believe others have it all together. Although, they may give the impression that everything is perfect no one is immune to the domineering effects of their mold. Famous people, political leaders, pro-athletes, you, and I have molds that have manipulated our existence. Keep what serves you and break away from your negative conditioning.

Your mold is comprised of many destructive beliefs. You have conditioned your mind to believe a number of things. Inside your stupid mold, you may have a belief that you are, for example, not good enough, not smart enough, unlovable, a phony, too tall, too short, too skinny, or overweight. Just as you negatively tricked your mind, you can positively condition your mind back to new beliefs. Remember that the first step to breaking away from limiting beliefs is to identify what they are and then destroy them. As an adult, I could see my father's insecurities yet was blind to the insecurities I inherited from my parents until I delved deep and started to recognize and decipher my divine messages. Become present to the messages from the Universe and discover what is there for you. Please don't dismiss intuitive nudges or you will miss out on a divine message from the Universe.

Knowledge and power are gained from every divine message that comes to you. I encourage you, to decipher the meaning behind the signals and take any necessary actions you are intuitively guided to take. Divine messages will help you discover who you are at your core, your true self, where you can live with passion and purpose. You will overcome limitations that keep you from living your best life and empower yourself with a new belief system that works for you, not against you.

This book is in your hands for a reason, whether you picked it up off the shelf because you were drawn to it, whether you received it as a gift, or saw that someone left it at a cafe, consider this in itself as a divine message! I am excited to be on this journey of transformation and self-discovery together. I want you to celebrate this moment, pat yourself on the back, for being the kind of person who is willing to get rid of limitations that sabotage you so you can improve your life. Go on, acknowledge yourself and give yourself a pat on the back, and continue reading.

5

EMOTIONS CATAPULTED
TO THE SURFACE

"Unexpressed emotions will never die.
They are buried alive and will come forth later in uglier ways."
– Sigmund Freud

In this chapter, I will share what happened when I was attacked. In later chapters, I will teach you what I learned about human behavior, including my own as a result of this incident. It has led to the discovery of a mold, a false identity that limited my entire existence. In the remainder of this book, I will teach you how to identify and break your mold and end the cycle of self-sabotage and limitation.

Following a night out at a friend's house, I drove home. It was a little after midnight. There was very little traffic on the road, and I noticed a black pickup truck with tinted windows behind me. The truck followed me through several traffic lights, and I began to wonder if I was being followed. As I got closer to home, I drove down obscure side streets, and the truck was still behind me. I became very cautious, I pulled into the entrance of the condo and watched to see if I was still being followed. To the left was the gate to the underground parking garage where I was headed. If the truck was still behind me, I planned to continue driving past the parking garage and up the hill which would take me back to the street. As I approached the gate, I watched as the black pickup truck turned right into a parking lot connected to the townhouse complex across the street from where I lived. I breathed a sigh of relief that the truck wasn't following me. I assumed the driver of the pickup was just going home.

I drove into the condominium's underground garage and parked in my designated spot. While I was gathering my things, I saw a man I didn't recognize walking briskly, so I waited in my car. I made a quick assessment and judged the man to be harmless. He was headed in the direction of the elevators and seemed to know where he was going, so I assumed he lived in the building. I briefly looked away to get my purse, and when I looked back up, he was gone. I looked in every direction, and there was no sign of him. I felt it was safe and got out of my car and I proceeded toward the elevators. I took out my key fob to open the door.

As I was halfway through the door, I heard footsteps running behind me. I thought it was someone wanting to catch the door before it closed, so for a split second, I held it open. The man I saw walking was now running towards me. When I saw the look on his face, I quickly realized he was coming for me. I tried to shut the door, but I was seconds too late, and he pushed his way through the door.

Without warning, he threw a punch with a closed hard fist to the top of my head. I could not believe what was happening. He repeatedly punched me in the head and face, and I was fighting to shield myself from his blows. It was difficult to avoid being hit because I was trapped in a tiny space between two sets of doors. There was one door from the parking garage and another directly across leading to the elevators.

He kept punching me and threw me up against the walls. I felt as if things were happening in slow motion. I was fighting as hard I could and trying to maintain some control and avoid being knocked to the ground. After a good struggle though, I lost the fight to stay standing. I never stopped fighting for one moment. He pinned me to the ground and was on top of me, but I refused to give in. I struggled beneath him, and whenever I freed my hand, I tried to hit his face, but he kept blocking my hand. He never said a single word. The only words I said were "Dear God! Help me!" I didn't yell because I was in a basement of the condo trapped between two doors and I knew that no one would hear me.

At one point, I managed to knee him hard in the groin. He didn't even flinch which led me to believe he was on drugs. I was in utter disbelief this was happening to me. Thoughts of my family went through my mind. My youngest niece was only two years old at the time, and the thought of never seeing her grow up was agonizing. I couldn't believe this was the way I was going to die, strangled and assaulted in an underground parking garage by a man I didn't even know. I couldn't fathom how someone who knew nothing about me or my life acted so violently toward me and was deliberately harming me.

As if a light switch went off, he got off me. When he stood up, he tried to kick me, but I managed to get out of the way. He tried to open the door, but it didn't budge. He didn't realize that you had to press the button on the wall to unlock the door. Instead, he opened the other door which was directly opposite and ran into the building to the elevators. The contents of my purse, my shoes, earrings, and cell phone were all strewn across the floor, I didn't want to waste even one second to pick up my belongings because I feared he might come back.

I ran barefoot into the parking garage and stepped on the rubber wire to open the garage door. There was no one in sight that could help me. The exit led to the back entrance of the building. My attacker was in the building, and I knew he had to exit from either the front or back doors. I had a fifty-fifty chance of running into him. I hid in the bushes at the side of the building in between the front and back doors so I could avoid running into him. Minutes later he ran past the front of the bushes I was hiding behind. I waited just long enough until I felt it was safe to get out from behind the bushes without him seeing or hearing me. I ran down the road to the 24-hour convenience store at the corner. It was the only place I knew for certain was open. The bright lights in front of the corner store brought me some sense of relief. I ran in and called 911.

I was taken to the hospital. I could barely move, my whole body was stiff from the stress of the fight. I had contusions to the head, and my face was swollen. My face swelled so quickly that the doctor believed my brain shifted from the force of the punches. He also suspected my cheekbones were broken; fortunately he was mistaken.

I was in a room at the hospital's Emergency Department terrified, confused and in a state of shock. The doctors, nurses, and police officers were in and out my room evaluating the situation, asking questions and sending me for tests. I got up from the hospital bed and walked to the bathroom. When I saw myself in the mirror, it was surreal, almost dream-like. I couldn't believe this was real. My face was so swollen I could barely recognize myself. I was horrified.

A police guard was stationed outside my room to protect me. After the hospital, I was taken to the police station to give my statement. The first time I was at the hospital, I couldn't remember being sexually assaulted. When I was a little more clearheaded, I knew I had been sexually assaulted, and from the police station, I was taken back to the hospital for more tests.

I laid down on the hospital bed in total bewilderment. I didn't call anyone to let them know what happened. I knew I didn't have the wherewithal to handle my own emotions let alone anyone else's. I was used to being the one in my family who supported everyone else, but I had no idea how to receive support in return.

I remember the police officers asking me several times throughout the night if they could get me something to eat. I was shuttled back and forth between the hospital and the police station and hadn't eaten anything all night, and they were encouraging me to have something. I had no appetite, but finally, I asked for a cup of tea. That's all I wanted. It was the quiet support and comfort that I needed and the only kind I knew how to accept. It required nothing in return. I didn't need to take care of it. I didn't need to console it. I didn't need to answer any questions or solve its problems. The warmth of the tea gave me momentary comfort as I struggled to make sense of what happened. The tea was like a soothing warm embrace I wouldn't admit to anyone that I desperately needed. I realized then that I was always looking for comfort in little things I could give myself because I didn't know how to accept comfort offered from the people in my life.

The police arranged to have a personal alarm system

installed in my home because I was considered to be at risk of being a victim of repeated violence. They feared my attacker would strike again, if not me then it would be someone else. I was given a device that fit on my keychain that I could press if I felt I was in danger. It would activate the alarm and immediately dispatch a 911 emergency. It's a valuable safety measure, but it didn't feel right for me. It actually made me feel more paranoid by having it. I felt it was a constant reminder of what happened. I felt unsafe every moment. I took what little control I had left and made arrangements to have it uninstalled. You are in charge of your healing in any situation you have gone through. You must listen to your intuition and take any measures you can to assist in your healing, even if it goes against what others say. True intuition will never steer you wrong.

The impact of being strangled caused my voice to be strained and raspy for several days. I was told to call 911 immediately if I had trouble breathing because symptoms may worsen and could potentially be fatal. When my friend suggested I get some fresh air we went for a short walk. After just a few minutes I was short of breath. Instead of disappointing my friend or telling him I was finding it hard to breathe I suggested we sit on a park bench. I was ignoring my needs and making others more important because it was a familiar pattern for me so once again, I kept what I was feeling to myself. You are important. Please don't neglect your needs for fear of upsetting someone.

My attacker was caught a few weeks later. I was told by police that "I got him good" which I have to admit, gave me huge satisfaction from hearing those words. He had bruises and scratches all over and indents from my fingernails on his arms. Apparently, his girlfriend told police she thought he was in a bar fight.

Internalizing my emotions became a behavioral pattern that I had developed over the years. I kept my emotions small by suppressing and ignoring them as much as possible. I was scared of my feelings and afraid of losing control. It felt as if, people around me were waiting for a bigger response from me and I kept waiting for the other shoe to drop. I had grown accustomed to taking shallow breaths or holding my breath as if bracing for the next disaster.

My body wasn't cooperating with my planned emotional avoidance. I was in a constant state of stress. I was hypersensitive to my surroundings and on high alert no matter where I was. I had no appetite and lost a substantial amount of weight in a very short time. Later, I was diagnosed with Post Traumatic Stress Disorder (PTSD). I suffered silently and kept my diagnosis from family and friends. There were times when it was obvious to those around me that something was wrong, but when anyone asked me if I was all right, I downplayed what I was feeling and said I was okay.

I didn't want to show my vulnerability. The level of emotion I felt was uncomfortable and unfamiliar. I didn't want to process what I was feeling, but I was also finding it extremely difficult to continue repressing it. I was terrified of getting trapped in my emotions because my feelings were so intense. I wondered if I would ever be able to recover once my buried emotions erupted. My emotional distress was compounded by physical symptoms. Like when my entire body would tense up, or I'd break out into a cold sweat because I heard the footsteps of a person walking from their car in a parking lot and it would take me back to my attack or when someone got too close to my personal space.

There was an older Asian man walking down the sidewalk, he had a small frame and what I saw instead at first glance was my attacker who was a much taller and larger framed Caucasian male who looked nothing like him. Physical reactions were brought on unexpectedly and beyond my control which was unsettling to me. I would unexpectedly break into a cold sweat, or feel sick to my stomach, thoughts would race through my head, and I suffered from headaches every day. Sometimes I would catch myself holding my breath and other times my heart would race so fast I thought the sound of it beating was palpable.

It felt like my mind and body were working against me, and I was anxious and stressed all the time. Every time before I would get into the car I would check the backseat to see if there was anyone hiding there. Then I'd get in, turn around, and even when it was obvious no one was there I still had to double check before I locked the doors. I wasn't dealing with my stress, so it was coming out through physical manifestations. My symptoms were telling me to release the stored trauma. My mind and body were actually working for me and not against me.

My emotions were in serious need of attention, and my body was not letting me ignore what was happening. Years of unprocessed emotions were catapulted to the surface, and I was forced to deal with what I was desperately trying to ignore. We all have emotions we try to bury or suppress. This is an ineffective and unhealthy way to manage your feelings.

I hoped that if I just ignored what happened and pretended that it wasn't a big deal, I could avoid feeling the overwhelming pain of what happened. If I allowed myself to feel the full extent of emotional pain I feared I wouldn't be able to keep things together anymore. I wondered if I would start to unravel the carefully controlled emotions I stored away like a locked filing cabinet that has no key.

I had worked really hard in the past to maintain tight control over my surroundings, and now I was fighting hard to maintain what was comfortable, familiar and safe to avoid a total breakdown. I felt as if the filing cabinet that represented my past and all my controlled emotions was pried open and the contents were scattered and got jumbled together. I wasn't sure how to start to put it all back together. It was as if I had to start reading the contents of each page and acknowledge my past in order to piece it all together.

I realized this was bigger than me and beyond what I

knew how to control. Not only was I worried about the present I was concerned about the future ramifications. In several years down the road would my suppressed feelings show up out of nowhere, unannounced and without warning to force me over the edge and lose control? Losing control of my emotions terrified me.

Several police officers suggested I get counseling and I had shrugged it off. It was obvious to them I was trying to ignore what happened. I was left to wonder if my future would be negatively impacted both emotionally and physically. Because of the trauma I sustained to the head I was told by the doctor it was possible I would have issues with cognitive function years down the road. My stress levels were high. Every time I had a bad headache I worried it was the sign of oncoming brain damage. I knew I had little or no control on what may or may not happen physically, but I did have the power to deal with my emotions, so I decided to get help and sought counseling.

I gradually began to share my experience with a few people, and although it felt uncomfortable and unfamiliar, I knew it was necessary to begin healing. In writing this book, I am sharing my experience and continuing the healing journey. I invite you to go on a healing journey. Ready to start? Just turn the page.

6

STAGNATION IS THE DEATH OF POSSIBILITY

"Iron rusts from disuse; stagnant water loses its purity, and in cold weather becomes frozen; even so does inaction sap the vigor of the mind."
– Leonardo da Vinci

It was time to take action, confront emotions and take back control of my life. So, I decided to get help from a professional counselor. Part of my counseling was acknowledging the unrecognized feelings and memories of my past that had silently sabotaged my existence. Emotions were now flooding in a constant stream demanding that I stop resisting them. Acknowledging buried emotions is your first step in the healing process. Processing intense feelings is an opportunity to heal from past traumas or hurts. Don't be afraid to connect with your emotions. Be willing to accept that good can come from suffering. I believe, the greater the trauma, the bigger the lesson. You must be open to the possibility of finding the lesson, or you will be blind to the rewards. Lessons and miracles are happening all around you every day. You need to believe they exist in order to see and experience them. A miracle is waiting for you. Believe it, expect it, and you will receive it.

Your mold represents who you think you are, not who you truly are. By changing just one of your faulty ingrained beliefs, you can change your entire self. You are then able to live more authentically and transform your life for the better. Your mold has you trapped in a false belief. Your thoughts, emotions, and actions are now dependent on those beliefs. At times, you fear taking action because of the lies you tell yourself based on your beliefs. You don't recognize it as a lie because you have been conditioned to believe your false story. Your life is molded and shaped by limiting beliefs. The world is not conspiring against you. View others and the Universe as friendly and having your best interest at heart. The Universe is on your side and is waiting for you to break your mold. Let's imagine you're going to an interview or an audition. It can be scary, but you want to go in with the attitude that everyone wants you to get the job or the part. The employer, director, and the casting agent all want you to get the gig. Act as if they are on your side instead of believing they are against you and judging you. It is easier for everyone if you are the perfect choice. Why can't it be you? Why assume they are against you? Why is someone else more worthy? Celebrate and act as if you got the job or the part.

When we are accustomed to thinking we're not good enough, and constantly beating ourselves up we automatically assume others are against us. The Universe is on your side. Adopt this belief and your limiting beliefs will start to shift to love and approval and you will find yourself living in ease vs. dis-ease. Your mold is like a group of diseased cells destroying the healthy cells of your mind and corrupting your thoughts.

Move forward and ignore any resistance to change. It requires courage to surpass one's limitations. The rewards are well worth the inevitable growth that follows. Inactivity of any kind is caused by fear. Fear kicks in and fearful thoughts dominate, and you avoid pain by not taking action. There is nothing to fear. Fear is simply a belief. You can achieve what you desire by taking action and moving forward and letting go of your fears.

Stagnation is the death of possibility. We can be stagnant and experience inactivity or staleness in jobs, in relationships, in personal growth. Movement is required to advance your potential and turn your dreams into a reality. When you take action to accomplish personal aspirations, you are in fact paving the path to personal empowerment.

There was a time when I was overwhelmed by the idea of writing a book. I wrote a mere few pages, which was not even a chapter and far from a book. I was overwhelmed by the thought of writing an entire book, so I broke it down to make it more manageable. I took action and created movement. First, I started with the ideas I wanted to share and then I broke it down from there, thought by thought and then chapter by chapter. The process became infinitely easier and within reach because I took action to move forward, even though I wasn't sure how I was going to do it.

If you take the necessary action to break your limitations, you can realize your potential and things in life will become less conflicted. You still need to apply effort and put in the work to get results, but the path to get there will become smoother, much clearer, and less prohibitive. Things you believed were impossible and unobtainable now become possible and tangible.

If you are struggling with something you wish to do or achieve, break it down into pieces and take some form of action to move ahead. I went from having the idea of writing a book into a finished product simply by starting the first few pages. When I first started, writing a book seemed impossible and just a dream. When I took action to actually write, something extraordinary happened in the process. The doubt vanished and was replaced with absolute certainty that I would finish the book. In fact, about halfway through the process, I was already gathering ideas for my next book. The dream of writing became a fixed reality. I started off not knowing if I could even manage writing one chapter to a strong knowing that I would write an entire book. You can stop stagnation and create movement by taking the necessary action to move from concept to results and turn your dreams into reality.

7

YOU ARE WORTHY. YOU ARE ENOUGH. YOU DESERVE.

"The biggest disease affecting humanity:
I'm not enough."
– Marisa Peer

The belief that you are not good enough is one of the most common and most destructive limiting beliefs. If you inherently believe you are not good enough, no matter what you do or accomplish, it will never feel like enough, and you will never be satisfied. You have created an expectation of yourself that you will always fall short of your standards. No matter what actions you take, you will consistently believe you can never do enough or be enough, no matter how hard you try. The truth is you already are good enough, but you can't see it. The simple daily habit of repeating the words

"I am enough" over time will make it impossible for your mind to argue otherwise. According to hypnotherapist Marissa Peer, "The biggest disease affecting humanity is: I'm not enough, and the way to get past it is to say I am enough out loud or silently."

We are all born worthy and deserve the best life has to offer, but somewhere along the way, we forgot the innate truth that we are all worthy. We became conditioned by our false beliefs. We are worthy beings, independent of our opinion or the opinion of others. We needlessly obsess about what others think of us. Other people's opinions of you, in no way, reflect who you really are. In fact, their opinions of you may be based on their own insecurities.

I was working for a company that hired a consultant who came to me and said: "You think you are better than you are." Now, I had been working for this company for many years and had gone through several upper management changes, and each one of them valued me and praised my work. The consultant was there a few months and was trying to make his mark before his contract expired. There is value in constructive criticism, and you may learn from what is being said however in this case I believe he was deliberately trying to offend, and belittle me. Trying to belittle someone because you want to feel better about yourself or gain the upper hand is coming from a place of insecurity, and you do not have to tolerate such behavior. Just because someone says something about you doesn't automatically make it true. He was deliberately trying to offend and I refused to accept it so, I replied, "I know I'm better than you think I am," and we moved on to something else. I would be lying if I said I wasn't hurt by what he said. At first, I took it very personally and questioned my abilities. The more I mulled over what he said, the more I realized his remark was unfounded. Effective leaders know how to inspire and uplift others they do not try to belittle, degrade, manipulate or overpower others. Effective leaders strive to empower you so you can deliver outstanding results. Don't believe what others say about you just because they say it. Look to see if you can glean something positive from the comment and improve yourself. Never let anyone diminish your worthiness, especially since their comments most likely stem from their own poor self-value.

When you feel unworthy, it's impossible to fully appreciate your accomplishments because you don't recognize them as accomplishments. No matter what you do or how much effort you put in, it will never feel like you've done enough of anything because you don't feel good enough. Feeling unworthy can be so deeply rooted that you end up ignoring or downplaying any wins or accomplishments only to feed your belief. Or, you don't even bother trying to go after what you want, be it a relationship, job or another goal because your inner critic tells you, you will fail anyway. You have a choice to change your behaviors or to stay the same. You must decide if you are going to be the victim or become the victor. How do you go from one to the other? You make a choice to do so and then direct your focus on what you want rather than on what you don't want.

If you have been playing the role of a victim, then you need to take responsibility for accepting the role. This is not about blaming yourself, it's about acknowledging your part in what happened and empowering yourself to make a change. Ask yourself how being a victim is serving you? What has been the benefit to you? What need are you fulfilling? Can you fulfill the same need by doing something positive instead? All of your experiences and choices have led you exactly to where you are at this point in time. Be kind and gentle with yourself and acknowledge your humanness. A victim is stuck and immobilized by obstacles and fears; while a victor can see the value in all experiences and takes action to move beyond them despite circumstance. Know that you can make a better choice by shifting your thoughts from victim to victor and take actions that honor your worthiness and are conducive to your evolution and well-being.

You can find the miracle in your challenges by searching for the deeper meaning. Try to view your challenges from a different perspective. When you change your view on how you look at a situation, you transform consciousness and can readily see benefits that were previously hidden. Changing your consciousness can be as easy as shifting one word like victim to victor. This seemingly small shift can turn your entire life around and bring results you never imagined possible.

During a Reiki healing session, a vision of a past birthday surfaced. It was my birthday, and my mother was excited to show me something. Since it was my birthday, I assumed it was for me. It was a gift, but it wasn't for me. It was for my eldest brother whose birthday was a few weeks before mine. My mother said she knew I wouldn't mind if he got a gift and I didn't because "I was very understanding." She was right I didn't need a gift, but I was crushed. I felt as if I was not enough. Everyone else was more important than me, and I was unworthy. I pretended I wasn't upset and smiled through holding on to the belief of not being good enough. Once again, my self-worth took a hit, and my mold continued to accumulate more negativity. I didn't need a gift, and I would have understood if my brother received a gift, on any day other than my birthday. What I said to myself was that other people were more important than me, so I made them more important by putting their needs ahead of mine. Always putting other people's needs before your own turns you into a people pleaser. Your tendency to appease others slowly creeps up, and it becomes difficult to recognize that you are sacrificing your wants and needs for the sake of others.

Incidents from your early past can have a stronger impact, on you and your life, than you realize. On the day of my First Holy Communion, I started off the day feeling excited, and by the end of the day, I felt worthless and unlovable. The church service began, and I was sitting with the rest of my class. At some point, there was a short pause in the service so our parents could present us with a candle. When my friend Linda's mother approached, she stroked her daughter's face and told her that she was proud of her and loved her. When my mother came to me, she leaned in close as if she was going to whisper something in my ear. I was expecting something similar to what my friend's mother said, but she handed me the candle and said: "Don't break the candle." My heart sank. I was crushed. My friend asked what my mother had said and when I told her she burst into laughter. To hide my embarrassment, I laughed along with her and pretended I wasn't hurt. Hiding my feelings became a pattern. When I was hurt, I pretended I wasn't, or I laughed to hide my pain. I interpreted my mother's words to mean that I wasn't important. A candle, an inanimate object, was more important than I was. I added more false beliefs to my mold, the beliefs that I was unworthy and unlovable. Because I felt others were more important than me I felt it was my job to be tough and take care of everyone else. So, I never let anyone know I was hurt or upset. Looking back, I recognize my First Holy Communion ceremony was important to my mother, and she expressed it in the way she knew how.

Often when we relive past experiences through the eyes of our younger selves, we continue to be emotionally impacted by the experience. I can go back to my communion day and relive the moment look back with adult eyes and not the eight-year-old who felt unworthy, and unlovable and change my view. My mother wasn't deliberately trying to hurt my feelings. She wanted to ensure she had a keepsake of an important day. My mother saved my communion day candle until the day she died. Incidentally, it never got broken.

If you look back at your experiences with adult eyes, you can dissolve the hurt associated with painful experiences. You can also give yourself what you needed at the time but didn't get. Did you want to feel you were worthy? Did you want to hear the words "I love you"? Did you want attention from a parent? Did you want your family to include you and make you feel wanted? Did you want a parent to praise you? Did you want to hear you were a good kid? Did you need affection? Did you want to feel needed? Go back and give yourself what you wanted, but were missing and change your perspective on the challenges of your past.

Shine Like The Golden Buddha

It is your time to shine like the Golden Buddha and awaken to your authentic self. In Thailand, a group of monks was relocating a ten-foot statue of Buddha weighing over five tons. When they moved the statue, it was dropped, and a beam of golden light glimmered through. When they took a closer look, they discovered it was plastered over, and there was something beneath. When the monks stripped away the plaster, they found a solid gold Buddha underneath. It is believed to have been covered to conceal its' true value so it would not be stolen. Like the plaster covering up the golden Buddha for 600 years, your mold, your false-self has been hiding your true innate worth from the world. Your inner light is eternal, but like the Golden Buddha statue, you have covered it with false beliefs. If you chip away the hardened layers of limitations, you will get back to source energy and unveil your innate gifts and inner light. Let your true self emerge illuminate as it was at birth, and feel the worthiness that is your truth.

One afternoon, when I came home from school, I noticed my mother was upset. I asked her what was wrong. She said she was angry with my dad. She told me she had enough and that she and I were going to leave. She made a plan that on the following Friday she and I would go away together. I didn't want to leave my dad and siblings, but I didn't know how to tell her without hurting her feelings, so I said nothing. I decided I would have to tell her on the day we were to leave that I didn't want to go. The dreaded day came, and nothing happened. My mother never said a word, and I didn't question it. We never spoke about it again. I kept our plan a secret from everyone, including my siblings. I learned that if I kept bad things a secret then by some miracle they would disappear and I could protect others from going through the pain I was experiencing. This created a pattern of hiding my suffering.

I don't believe my mother really intended on leaving. She was looking for validation. She needed to know I loved her more than everyone else or at least enough to go with her. One of her childhood beliefs was feeling unworthy of love. She was considered the black sheep of her family and felt as if she didn't belong. Her belief was buried deep inside her mold and dominated her actions. Validation comes in many forms, and we all seek it from time to time. My mother was looking for validation by trying to secure love that was withheld from her as a child. She needed to feel like she was the favorite if only for a brief moment. If you can remove limiting beliefs and feel your own worthiness, you won't need external validation from others.

Life requires that you go after your wins; however, most people give up just before they get to the finish line. You shrink back when life gets too tough, or you sabotage yourself because you feel like you didn't deserve your past successes, or feel that you won't succeed at anything in the future. I was on the track and field team in elementary school and competing in a long-distance race against several contending schools. Although it is suggested that you should pace yourself for a long-distance run, I didn't think I would be able to catch up so when the start gun was fired, I ran as fast as I could. This gave me a strong lead over most of the runners. My teacher and track coach was standing on the sidelines and cheering me on shouting "Go Kolar! Go Kolar! Kolar! Go Kolar!" I had no idea that he would be there at the halfway point cheering me on. I was taken aback by the support, but I loved it. As I headed around the bend, I noticed two girls running in tandem behind me. I slowed down and motioned for them to go ahead of me. They looked puzzled. I slowed down even more and once again, motioned for them to pass me. They shrugged, and at my insistence went ahead of me. I was doing too well for my conditioned brain to allow. I was telling myself I didn't deserve to win. I decided the two strangers behind me were better and faster and deserved to win, so I ensured they had an advantage over me by letting them pass when we got to the bend in the track that way no one saw me slow down.

I was so close, yet I let them win because putting others first was familiar to me. I felt I didn't deserve to win. It was another block to my best self. Don't hesitate to showcase your best self because of the belief that others are better or more deserving. Be your best self now and don't diminish your gifts. The universe is abundant therefore it is unnecessary to relinquish your success, happiness or talents for the sake of others. Success and happiness are available to you if you don't give both up to others. Don't give away what belongs to you and is rightfully yours because you don't feel deserving of it. You deserve the best life has to offer. You are perfect just the way you are. Be accepting and allow your rewards. You are worthy. You are enough. You deserve.

We have a tendency to define an outcome even before it begins based on our beliefs about what should happen. Don't set yourself up for failure before you even begin. I decided I shouldn't win the race so I consciously assured that outcome. It didn't feel good letting the runners in ahead of me because I knew I was better than what I placed and I knew my teacher would have been disappointed if he knew what I had done. My self-sabotage was suspended at the beginning of the race because I forgot that I wasn't supposed to win. When I got close to the finish line, the realization came back. Once again, I was being controlled by limiting beliefs and sabotaged my success, so I created an outcome befitting of my thoughts, patterns, behaviors, and beliefs.

It's surprising how many seemingly insignificant experiences in your past continue to impact the present and your future. When I was a kid, I accidentally locked myself in my aunt and uncle's bathroom. The doorknob came off in my hand, and I couldn't get it back on. I yelled for help, but no one heard me. I was probably only in there for no more than a few minutes, but it seemed like hours. Eventually, my aunt came to my rescue. She told me there was a trick to opening the door and walked me through it. I was asked why I didn't yell for help. I said I did, but no one heard me. My aunt's friend admitted she heard something but thought it was the kids playing in the basement. I believed it was my fault the doorknob came off and also that no one could hear me… if only I were louder…. if only I weren't so rough with the doorknob. And of course, I blamed myself for being stupid for not knowing the trick to opening the door.

Recognizing Your Own Value

How can you expect others to recognize your value if you don't recognize your own? Your beliefs are like mirrors reflecting back at you all areas of your life. For example, I felt unworthy and my dating life reflected that. I immediately turned down men without giving anyone a chance. One day when I met a man at a coffee shop. He asked if he could put his briefcase on one of the chairs at my table, and asked if I would watch it while he stood in line to grab a coffee. In the meantime, a couple of my friends came back to the table, and he noticed, so he popped out of line and removed his briefcase to free the chairs at my table. He placed it back at his and thanked me. Several minutes later I went to look at some cards at the adjoining book store. My friend told me he was staring at me. I looked over, and sure enough, he was staring at me and smiling. I smiled back and continued reading the greeting cards. Next, my friend said, "He's coming this way, I bet he wants to ask you out." When I saw him heading toward me, I panicked. I was terrified he was going to ask me out. My first instinct was to run, so that's exactly what I did. I ran out the front doors of the book shop - in my high heels.

Looking back, I realize my reaction was extreme. Rather than running from him, I was really running from myself and my happiness. He was handsome, tall and based on his attire and demeanor appeared to be a professional businessman. I thwarted any good that could have come from the exchange. Can you think of a time where you have been running from yourself? What happiness are you blocking from your life? I implore you to find it and stop running from yourself. When you develop an awareness of the blocks you have, you can release them all. Awareness is the first step. You can start by looking at what's not working in your life and questioning why it isn't working. Be boldly honest as you discover what controls your actions and behaviors.

When you consistently put the needs of others first, your own needs slowly become invisible. You end up with no time or space left for you. When you find yourself overwhelmed by the burden of other people's problems, worries, upsets, disappointments, and challenges you must pull back and make yourself a priority. It is essential that you carve out some space and time for yourself, mentally and physically, even if it is a tiny space or a short time. Creating space for yourself could be as simple as having a bubble bath, calling a friend, reading a magazine, indulging in your favorite dessert, sipping a glass of wine, getting your nails done, sitting on a park bench, going for a walk, listening to your favorite music. How about claiming a comfy chair as your own that no one else gets to sit in, or staking out a little spot in a room or dedicating an entire room to yourself with all your favorite things in that room, like your hobbies, collections, books, fill it with everything that you like. Even the tiniest space you create for yourself can lift some of the pressure and allow you to relax and breath and not feel guilty about it. Assisting others is noble and rewarding. However, when it monopolizes all your time and takes over your well-being you need to re-evaluate the situation so you can avoid feeling overburdened, unappreciated, and undervalued.

Always putting the needs of others first is a symptom of self-neglect. It's an excuse for avoiding your own needs and feelings. You are the most important person in your life. You must put yourself first and understand that it's not selfish to put yourself first. When you do, you give your best self to others. By ignoring your feelings, you teach others it is acceptable to disregard or overlook your feelings. You are training them how to treat you. Teach them to recognize your value.

Growing up, my mother was a stay at home mom and babysat to earn extra money. I can remember watching her and admiring how she cared for and played with the kids. She was genuinely loving and kind towards the kids. As I watched her, I wished I could remember being their age. I wondered how she treated me. Did she have the same kind of love for me when I was younger? Did that kind of love even exist for me? The kind of sweet, nurturing love she showered on the kids she took care of. I wondered what it would be like to feel that kind of unconditional love. Was unconditional love always there but I was unable to see it because I was somehow blocking it? My parents would show that same doting love to their grandkids. My parents adored them and talked about their grandkids all the time. They carried photos of each of them in their wallets and shared them at every opportunity.

When you feel inadequate, it is difficult to see the love that surrounds you. It could be there, but you fail to recognize and receive it. I never knew my grandparents but wondered what it would be like to have grandparents that had unconditional love for you? What was it like to feel good enough because they wanted to do something nice for you, take you to the park, give you money, show up for your school plays, take you to swimming classes, guide you, encourage you, support you or answer your questions?

You may or may not have had a loving role model in your life. You don't need others to treat you well in order to feel loved, successful or feel worthy. Love is an inside job. You must love yourself. Always remember that you were born worthy and loveable. It's important to be loved by others, and I am not implying it isn't, however, if you feel unconditional love is lacking from your life you can give it to yourself or surround yourself with the right people who are capable of loving you.

Often, you may feel that there is something you need to do first in order to feel worthy of love. When I finish this task, I will be loveable. When I am perfect, I will love myself. When I achieve or do something, I will feel lovable. There is nothing you need to do in order to be worthy of love or to love yourself. When you love the person you are despite your flaws and learn to love the parts of yourself you don't like then you also make it so much easier for others to love you.

You may not have had anyone take you to a ball game, hockey practice, swimming lessons, a movie, dinner or to give you advice or cheer you on. You may have felt neglected, alone, and lonely, but it certainly doesn't mean you were unworthy or unlovable. You have to do the job of giving yourself what you need or recognize that others are trying to love you in the only way they know how. Don't let the words, actions or inactions of others determine if you are lovable or let it define what you believe about yourself. It is never too late to start learning to love yourself. Never give up on you. You can love yourself when you feel unlovable by repeatedly telling yourself what you most need to hear. What words do you need to hear that you never heard in the past? Tell yourself that you are a good son or daughter, or you love yourself or are proud of your accomplishments.

When I was in grade six, I taught myself how to swim by showing up and splashing around at the outdoor pool in my friend's condo almost every day for an entire summer. Showing up and consciously deciding to take action is an act of self-love. If you get into the flow of living your authenticity and unleash your potential the possibilities and successes and what you can achieve are limitless.

My parents never showed up for any of soccer practices or came to any of my games. It was easy for me to interpret that as meaning I wasn't important or lovable. Be mindful of your thoughts because your thoughts create your reality. Don't turn the situation into something it isn't. There may be a simple reason why things have or haven't happened. My dad worked long hours and weekends to support his family, and my mother was busy taking care of the family and home and didn't drive so she would have needed my father to take her. I had no expectations of them showing up because buried in my subconscious I was unworthy of having the support. One day, my sister Nancy showed up to watch one of my soccer games. I was running down the field striking the ball in front of me, and I could hear her cheering me on from the sidelines. It felt great but unfamiliar. I grew accustomed to not having support, but at the time I didn't realize the support I craved was inside me all along. If you don't have anyone cheering you on, be your own cheerleader in whatever you do. I grew up having very little expectations of people and conditioned myself to avoid being rejected or let down. I felt it was my job to give to others and when it came to getting support, I felt I had to do it myself.

One evening, my parents showed up to my school play. My father didn't have to work, so the whole family came to support me. Their support meant a lot to me, and I soaked in their presence. I decided at that moment that I was lovable, but the truth is I was always worthy of love, and so are you. At the end of the play, I received a standing ovation for my performance, and I was on a total high. That was a pivotal moment in my life because I finally felt worthy of love. However, I associated that I had to do something extraordinary in order to prove my worth and be loved. There is nothing that you need to do, be, or prove, to be worthy of love. You are and always will be lovable.

If you don't have people around that are capable of

guiding you, supporting you or loving you, then you need to learn how to give yourself the needed guidance, love and support. When you do, you will find people will show up in your life who can give you the love and assistance you need. The love, encouragement and the support you crave will come pouring in. Being your own cheerleader means you recognize your value by choosing to acknowledge and praise your accomplishments. Promote an environment for yourself that guides you to success and happiness. Give yourself a spiritual high five for making it this far. Stay positive and encourage yourself like you would a loved one, friend or teammate.

You can achieve your goals by staying committed to being your own best ambassador and cheerleader. Cheer yourself on from the sidelines of your life with unending encouragement and support. Treat yourself with the dignity, respect, and admiration you deserve.

The person you criticize the most, are angriest with, often upset with, disrespect the most and praise the least is you. Why are you being so hard on yourself? People will come and go, but you will be a constant presence. You are the most important person in your life. Treat yourself with love, honor, respect, and kindness.

Be happy, stand proud, jump, dance, praise your successes and be your best self. Your thoughts and actions will either promote success or keep you in a state of stress. Success brings you closer to your best self and stress pushes you further away. Things may not always be the way you want them to be, but you can always keep your spirit strong by supporting yourself. So go on and get out there and start actively scoring the goals of your life whatever they may be, and jump back up if you happen to stumble.

8

ACCEPTING COMPLIMENTS USING THE ACT

"I can live for two months on a good compliment."
— *Mark Twain*

We naturally seek the praise of others. Compliments are meant to make you feel good. The problem is we don't know how to accept compliments because our mold tells us we are inferior and not worthy of the compliment. So, we dismiss the praise and any of the good feelings that would have come with it. Instead of feeling good we end up feeling insignificant. How do you react to compliments? Can you graciously accept compliments or do you reject the good intentions by deflecting praise or react by criticizing yourself?

It is impossible to genuinely accept praise from others if you are in the habit of belittling yourself. A well-intentioned compliment meant to elicit good feelings instead triggers your inner critic. You conjure up a list of reasons why the compliment doesn't apply to you or why you don't deserve it. Or, you believe the person who gave you the compliment is lying or being sarcastic, and you end up feeling perhaps more insignificant instead of feeling complimented.

If you can honestly receive a compliment with ease, congratulations, you have a healthy level of self-value. Conversely, if you instinctively follow up a compliment with a self-deprecating, self-destroying remark, a reaction from your inner critic, then you are in what I call Killing Compliment Mode (KCM). This is when you battle against the compliment to obliterate it. When you battle and obliterate compliments, you downplay or reject them. You have an internal battle with yourself to prove the compliment was a mistake. Therefore, you end up rejecting or downplaying the compliment. Why would you want to obliterate compliments? You do this because feeling insignificant is familiar and feels comfortable, don't you? Ways in which you may downplay or reject compliments is by invalidating them or invalidating the person who gave you the compliment or simply ignoring them.

Your mold is at work in the subconscious trying to maintain the status quo of your beliefs. You've spent a lifetime being critical of yourself, so it's easy for your mind to come up with reasons to continue feeling insignificant and undeserving. This is a destructive pattern that feeds low self-esteem. If you have difficulty accepting compliments you must work to boost your self-esteem and change your limiting pattern.

If you find it difficult to accept compliments you no doubt find it easier to give praise to others, oddly enough, even to those you don't personally know. You must learn to recognize, acknowledge your successes and celebrate your achievements. You can learn to quiet your inner-critic by accepting and validating compliments. Make it a choice now to change your negative pattern and feel worthy of accepting the compliments you receive. When you stop KCM, you will be less self-critical and learn to appreciate and accept yourself in the process.

Feelings of unworthiness lie at the heart of not being able to freely accept compliments. When you feel less than or not good enough no matter how many compliments you receive you will not believe them to be true. You believe if the person who complimented you had all the facts and knew the truth about you they wouldn't be complimenting you at all. You may even go so far as to blame yourself for deceiving them in some way which led to a bogus or unfounded compliment.

Not accepting compliments is a form of self-rejection and another way we perpetuate feeling insignificant. With this behavior, you won't feel good enough no matter what others tell you or how many compliments you receive. You may even sabotage yourself and project to be less than the person you are so that you let others be superior to you. Then you become self-deprecating to a fault. I had a habit of always pointing out my flaws. When I was given a compliment, my natural instinct was to counter it with a negative. For example, when I was complimented on how straight my teeth were I would fire back with "thank you, but you should see my bottom teeth, they're really crooked," and then I would pull my bottom lip back to unveil two, slightly overlapping teeth that were not otherwise visible. "I love your outfit" would warrant a reply like "Oh, it was cheap, I bought it on sale, it's really old" and lastly, "I love your hair," "Thanks but it's really dried out, it's so flat and won't hold a curl."

When I was seventeen, the chef of the restaurant I waitressed at kindly suggested to me that when given a compliment I should just say thank you and leave it at that. He noticed I always obliterated any compliments. I never thought about how I accepted compliments before. When I did, I realized I wasn't capable of receiving flattery and had a habit of putting myself down. The putdowns and abusive self-talk were so deeply ingrained in my subconscious I didn't even know they existed. Although I was oblivious to my KCM tendency, it was obvious to the chef. When I examined my reaction when complimented I realized I belittled myself because in my eyes I was flawed. I wasn't perfect and felt I didn't deserve the compliment. Instead of accepting the praise I fed into the belief that I was unworthy and therefore was incapable of responding with a simple "thank you."

You may feel the need, to be honest about your flaws and imperfections. It's just limited thinking that's trying to solidify your insecurities. You can easily make the change to soak up flattery and boost your self-esteem. The first step is to look at your behavior and take note of how you react to flattery? Do you feel uncomfortable or undeserving? Get busy being nicer to yourself by stopping the abusive self-talk and stop rejecting the idea that you are worthy. Build your self-esteem. By bringing awareness to your reaction, you can immediately stop obliterating compliments and any self-disparaging remarks running through your mind and begin to accept compliments graciously.

Compliments, when graciously accepted, are gifts for both the giver and receiver. When you disparage the compliment aloud, you reject the gift and invalidate the person who complimented you by making them feel awkward for praising you. Do you seek praise from others by pointing out your strengths to validate your own self-worth? No matter how much praise you are given it is never enough if you feel undeserving and unworthy of it. Satiate your need for validation by praising yourself and believing it. You may overcompensate for lacking self-worth with a false confidence that shows up as cockiness or an inflated ego. In order to protect yourself, you may put up a front pretending that you don't care what others think.

Avoid the temptation to compare yourself to others. Comparing yourself to anyone is a lesson in futility;

after all what if they aren't as perfect as you think? There will always be someone better looking than you and someone not as good looking, someone more successful and someone less, someone wealthier and someone poorer. Learn to accept yourself as you are without comparing yourself to others and graciously accept compliments.

You can inch your way out of KCM and build a healthy level of self-esteem by using the following Accepting Compliment Technique (ACT). This technique is designed to make accepting compliments familiar to you. The more frequently you do the ACT, the easier it will become.

ACT Exercise

Every time you find yourself rejecting a compliment, take the compliment and make it bigger. Make the compliment as grand as you like; the bigger, the better, as if you're blowing up a balloon a big balloon. Do this even if you don't believe the words to be true. Your limitless mind will believe anything you tell it through repetition. When you magnify the compliment, it makes the original praise seem more plausible, and you will then be more likely to agree with it.

Get into the habit of making every compliment you receive bigger. Exaggerate the compliment and then repeat the original compliment and say the words "I am remarkable" at the end of it. Say it aloud, and with emotion. By adding emotion, you allow the words to resonate with you. This process helps you to become familiar with accepting and believing compliments and helps lessen the feeling that you're insignificant. The more you do it, the easier it will become to not only accept compliments but also believe that they are true.

This exercise works best if you say it aloud or write it down on paper. However, if you are doing this technique in the presence of others, I suggest doing it silently, so you are not distracted by their reaction.

Here are some examples of how to use the ACT:

Original Compliment: "You look beautiful."
Exaggerated Compliment: "I am a vision of beauty. I am beautiful on the outside and equally as beautiful on the inside."
ACT response: "I look beautiful. I am remarkable."

Original Compliment: "You have an impressive work ethic."
Exaggerated Compliment: "I am super productive and know how to get things done. There is no one that is more tenacious than I am."
ACT response: "I have an impressive work ethic. I am remarkable."

Original Compliment: "You are really smart."

Exaggerated Compliment: "I am a genius with a brilliant mind and sharp wit."
ACT response: "I am really smart. I am remarkable."

You must learn to appreciate your worthiness to recognize your value. That's when things will really shift for you. People can compliment you all day long, but it is much better to recognize and appreciate your own worth. When you learn to genuinely accept compliments, ironically, you won't need validation from others when you have an unshakeable belief in yourself.

Occasionally, you may slip back into KCM and deflect praise. However, you will be less critical of yourself when you stop killing compliments, and any setbacks will be temporary. You can change your reaction and emotions by first witnessing your behavior and then letting go of any self- deprecating thoughts. You can easily make the switch from KCM to living with praise when you commit to it. Remember, you were born extraordinary. If you just cringed at my compliment or insulted yourself, stop killing compliments and go back and reread this chapter!

9

GIFTS FROM YOUR
GREATEST TEACHERS

*"It has been said that something as small as the flutter of a butterfly's
wing can ultimately cause a typhoon halfway around the world."*
– Chaos Theory

Never underestimate the influence of your presence, words, actions, and inactions. For we create a ripple effect through all that we do and even through all that we don't do. As the chaos theory suggests, one small action can have an enormous causative effect. Similarly, an individual can be your greatest teacher and be unaware of the impact and transformation they have inspired in your life. In fact, you can be one of the greatest teachers in someone's life and be oblivious to the influence you have had in their life.

There are people around us who have immeasurably

transformed our lives and become tremendous teachers; whether they intended to teach us something or not. It is often during times of our greatest challenges that these teachers suddenly appear, in time it seems, to inspire a breakthrough within us so that we may evolve to our highest potential. These teachers can be anyone you know or have come in contact with. They can also be someone you never met or most likely will never meet. You don't have to know someone personally to be moved, touched, influenced, or inspired by them. They can act as a mentor or role model at a distance simply based on the knowledge you've gained, whether directly or indirectly, through their experiences.

Who has been your greatest teacher? One of the greatest and most cherished teachers in my life is my older brother Henry. I have learned a great deal from him throughout the years. He is one of the kindest and most thoughtful people I have had the privilege of knowing. He is a caring and compassionate soul and would never intentionally hurt anyone's feelings. Unfortunately most people would not get to know how extraordinary Henry is because he has a mental illness. He was diagnosed with schizophrenia in his teens. He suffered from hallucinations and at times was delusional and he required medications to lessen these symptoms. Some of the medications were effective while others failed to help. Schizophrenia is considered to be an incurable mental disorder which requires lifelong treatment in order to control symptoms and for one to function in society with minimal impairment. Most people only see his illness and dismiss him as a person worth knowing, or being around. This couldn't be further from the truth. We can be quick to judge others and draw conclusions about who they are without any real evidence to substantiate those conclusions. We base our conclusions on preconceived notions, which are influenced by falsehoods, fears, beliefs, and misunderstandings.

We all make unfair assumptions at times. I am certain we've all offended someone, intentionally or unintentionally, from a lack of understanding, compassion or connection. Like those who dismiss Henry's worthiness, we often dismiss our own worthiness and contributions just as carelessly. I encourage you to learn from everyone, even those you think you will not benefit from. And never underestimate your own contribution to family, friends, society, and the world because you never know when you have given someone the gift they needed most and had become one of their greatest teachers.

I remember it was as if my brother's illness happened over night. If there were any telltale signs leading up to it, I don't remember them. One day, totally unprovoked he started yelling obscenities over and over while in the shower. It was obvious something was very wrong. A friend of mine was over at the time, and she started laughing. I was mortified by what just happened, embarrassed, and hurt by my friend's reaction. To hide my feelings, I laughed along with her. There was nothing funny about the situation, and I felt like a horrible person for laughing. The belief I was a horrible person and the guilt that accompanied it added to the beliefs in my mold. My friend's laughter prompted me to keep my brother's illness a secret. I felt I needed to protect my brother from being laughed at. I was confused by what happened, and I was ashamed of myself for laughing with my friend.

My brother's illness grew progressively worse from that day. He was in and out of the hospital. He was never the same and quite frankly, neither was I. I wished I could have my brother back the way he was. His illness caused him to act in unpredictable and inappropriate ways. When he was doing well there was always an underlying feeling it wouldn't last. I found myself constantly waiting for the other shoe to drop.

Doctors at the hospital, where my brother was a patient, called a meeting with my family. The doctors felt they couldn't do anything more for him and suggested we put him in a group home for people with similar mental health issues. One doctor asked what we thought. No one in the room spoke. There was nothing but silence. The silent pauses were the moments we all needed to stuff down the emotions we were fighting back from erupting. At that moment, although I was just a kid I felt I had to be my brother's advocate so eventually, I spoke out and said I thought it was a good decision for my brother. Everyone else either nodded or said they agreed. I was broken but wouldn't admit it, not even to myself, so I put on a brave face. I created a belief that I was responsible for my brother's happiness and well-being. I was overwhelmed with having that responsibility, but I was accustomed to repressing my emotions, so no one in the room knew how I felt.

I often avoided talking about my brother and telling people about his illness because the thought of anyone judging him, making fun of him, treating him with disrespect, taking advantage of him, or mistreating him in any way was unbearable. I was trying to control the uncontrollable, and prevent the unforeseeable. I felt that my brother was cheated out of having a "normal life," a life devoid of mental illness and the challenges and stigma associated with the disorder. I felt guilty that Henry was sick and I wasn't. For years, I downplayed my successes and avoided opportunities. I considered my successes as an unfair reminder that Henry lacked the same opportunities I had. I held myself back and played small because of the enormous guilt I felt. Life was unfair, and I tried to equalize it. I deliberately cheated myself by creating obstacles and disadvantages when there were none. Think to yourself, are there obstacles or disadvantages you have created for yourself? If so, you must consciously choose to let them go. Even if you created them with good intentions, there is no benefit to you in holding yourself back and playing smaller than you are.

Henry has carved a special place in this world for himself just as he is. I consider him a walking earth angel who is meant to teach the world compassion and understanding. His teaching spans beyond the scope of family and friends with a reach that has no limits. My brother's illness has been simultaneously my greatest challenge and my greatest reward. When I look at the magnitude of his purpose in life, I can make peace with his illness and know it serves a higher purpose. I am beyond grateful for the gift of my brother and the lessons he has taught me. He has taught me empathy, love, compassion, patience, and how to move forward when faced with adversity. I love him unconditionally and can look past his illness and see his greatness. I have been given one of the greatest gifts possible, and his name is Henry. My wish for you is that you move forward through your challenges and consider yourself a lucky benefactor to receive gifts from your greatest teachers.

As human beings, we are constantly learning and evolving. Rather than considering challenges as the worst things that have happened and letting this negatively affect you, instead let the challenges provide the gift of awareness and insight. You can learn and grow from all your challenges knowing your greatest teachers are part of your life for your greater good. Reframe how you look at the less than perfect moments of your life. I promise there is a lesson if you will open your eyes long enough and wide enough to see the gift in the challenges you face.

There are painful experiences and circumstance in life that you wish never happened or that you didn't have to go through, and that you wouldn't wish upon anyone else but if you look at these challenging experiences, you will find they contain invaluable life lessons. Although I can't take away my brother's illness, I can reframe my thinking and be grateful for the lessons he has taught me. There are numerous gifts within the challenges we face. The gift may be to teach you how to be courageous, to be compassionate, to be empathetic, to let go of criticisms or judgments, to uplift others, to love, or to live an authentic life. These are all valuable lessons and tools for a better life. If you reframe and embrace your challenges, you will scale down the negative emotions that prevent you from seeing the benefit in your trials.

Your greatest teachers provide lessons very different from what you'd expect. Although what appears for you may not be what you had in mind it is what is necessary at that moment; a blessing disguised as a strange and unexpected gift. These often soul-shaking, life-altering gifts can teach you a great deal about life and human behavior including your own. They provide deep insight into your way of being, triggering an awareness into the motivation behind your actions helping you understand why you do the things you do and guide you to reflect on everything that has happened in your life. Through this self-reflection, you are guided to look beyond the limited conditioning of your past. We all face obstacles. It's how you handle these obstacles that will determine the quality of your life. If you reframe your thinking about your obstacles and stop resisting challenges, you will find the deeper awareness and value in them.

The Universe is always observing, listening and providing what is essential to your evolution. Failing to see the value in negative experiences is like rejecting a gift that has been offered to you. Instead of casting aside the gift accept it and appreciate the contents no matter how unexpected, painful, difficult or seemingly useless the contents may be. Despite the strange packaging, it may be the most valuable gift you have been given from one of your greatest teachers.

10

HEALING THE
MIND AND BODY

"The pains you feel are messengers. Listen to them."
– Rumi

D
isease or dis-ease is a coping mechanism for the body. The body is trying to purge toxic thoughts and emotions trapped in the body. The buildup of emotional toxins, when left unchecked, eventually manifest as illness. Dis-ease is a signal that emotions have been neglected for too long. The body is in a state of overwhelm and asking for help. It's fighting back by sending an SOS by way of aches, pains, or disease. The dis-ease signal is a call for healing. If you ignore the signals, it will worsen. One must manage the physical and mental pain before it gets to a point where

one can no longer control it. By healing our minds, we can heal our bodies.

Toxicity in the body can be caused by a myriad of negative emotions and states of being, for instance, stress, anxiety, low self-esteem, hatred, repressed anger, frustration, fear, guilt, and sadness. When we are experiencing pain, we could ask ourselves "What are you thinking about right now?" I believe healing lies in changing how you feel and think about your illness or disease. Spiritual wellbeing can be the key to physical wellbeing. The treatment, in part, depends on the thoughts and feelings you have towards what ails you. It is imperative that we take care of our mental selves so that we avoid or minimize illness and disease while it's manageable. View illness in your body as an opportunity to change your thinking and how you feel. Do you notice how your body reacts when stressed? You may suffer from headaches, back pain or feel tension and tightness in muscles in the neck and shoulders. These can be the first distress signs to alert you and a push to take some action to change it and to seek help.

Negative thoughts and feelings are a breeding ground for illness. Constant stress is physically and emotionally destructive and when ignored for long periods can turn into something serious. If you have been diagnosed with a serious illness, it can be extremely difficult to get out of the negative mindset and change your thinking. Please don't wait too long to help yourself. This is not intended as medical advice, and you should always seek the advice of a medical professional. However, you can do what is in your power and change your thoughts and beliefs about your illness.

Placebos or sugar pills have been proven to be effective because the patient believes and expects the placebo to be effective. Their thoughts were focused on the placebo working for them and although it was just a sugar pill, saline injection or other treatment with no medicinal properties some patients experienced health benefits. This is what is known as the placebo effect. Often, placebos have been administered in clinical trial purposes, and although there was no intended therapeutic benefit, it rather provided a psychological change in some patients. This is a good example of how your thoughts and attitudes can greatly influence your health and how you handle illness.

We must purge toxic people and situations from our lives to avoid the mental and physical impact of absorbing their negative energy. Some people leave you feeling drained and empty and contribute nothing uplifting, nothing positive. In fact, they may deliberately want to manipulate you and bring you down. In this case, you must avoid contact or at least limit contact with them. It may be impossible to limit contact with someone if they are close to you. In this case, you will have to create new boundaries based on what you will tolerate.

Energy vampires will suck the energy out of you at every opportunity. You are then guaranteed to feel drained, exhausted or unsettled. The same can be felt from being around someone who incessantly gossips or puts others down. We all have encountered people who don't make us feel good after being with them. These are people who incessantly complain, gossip, and find fault with everyone and everything. You end up feeling ill at ease and spent after interacting with them. We all must limit contact to avoid feeling the negative impact.

If energy vampires are closely connected or related to you it may be virtually impossible to avoid them; however, you can teach them a new way of interacting with you by setting healthy boundaries on what you will or will not tolerate. Don't give away all your emotional energy. Instead, you can teach people how you want to be treated so you can avoid feeling chronically fatigued or getting your positivity drained out of you.

Our surroundings are a reflection of our state of mind and can greatly affect our mood and impact our quality of life. Clutter in the home clutters up the mind. If you are surrounded by chaos, you will create mental chaos, what I refer to as mind clutter. You may not be the most organized person in the world but clearing the chaos around you creates space for new opportunities to enter your life. Donate your belonging or gift it to friends. You will feel lighter and clearer. If there is an item of clothing in your closet you haven't worn for a season in all likelihood, you will never wear it again. If you keep clothes you know you will never wear because you cannot bear to part with them, ask yourself what you are holding on to. Is there a link to the past you don't want to give up? Do you connect emotions with clothes you're holding on to?

You can't move on to a new chapter in your life when you're repeating the same one over and over. You must learn to let go of unnecessary attachments. You may be holding on to things for negative reasons and use things like reminders or even for self-punishment. Are you holding on to who you were in the past? Are you punishing yourself because you feel guilty about the past and need reminders so you can continue to play out the story that you are a bad person?

Declutter your surroundings to free yourself from mind clutter and past attachments. Clearing your space will cut the invisible cord that ties you to the past. If you clear your closet, you can clear your mind and emotions as well. It can be difficult to get rid of items you have a strong emotional attachment to but if you consider the amount of joy your belongings would bring to someone else it will be easier to give them up.

You are the creator of your life. Create a healthy environment for yourself by clearing your emotions and your space. Develop a supportive environment and don't let anyone steal your energy. Others can only do that if you let them. Subconsciously, you may willingly give away your energy, so you protect yourself by not sharing your true self. You are in complete control of the image you choose to project to others. You often choose to portray yourself in different ways depending on who you're with. You keep certain behaviors from some people, while in other relationships you highlight those same behaviors. It may be instinctual to protect ourselves; however, problems arise when we do it so often we become a false version of who we truly are. When this happens, you relinquish control, and you stop making decisions that are in your best interest. Instead of hiding who you are, learn to free your true nature and let true self emerge no matter who you happen to interact with.

You may compartmentalize yourself and hide certain behaviors or characteristics as a way of avoiding judgment and protecting yourself. For example, you may have a different persona in a work setting versus personal life or behave differently with a particular group of friends in order to avoid being singled out for having differing views. Do not judge yourself, and do not fear the judgment of others towards you. You must learn to accept yourself as you are. We are all here on our own journey. Embrace your uniqueness and don't be afraid to show your authentic self to anyone. It is paramount that you speak up and stand up for yourself and don't let others drain your energy, or treat you poorly because you think you're inferior or don't want to hurt their feelings because you value theirs above your own. You are the most important person in your life, it's time to acknowledge it and put your needs first. It is liberating when you can speak your truth and express who you truly are.

"Be empty of worrying. Think of who created thought! Why do you stay in a prison when the door is so wide open."
– Rumi

Fear is a mind-made prison that keeps you shackled to an inferior self. Fear, worry, doubt and self- sabotage keeps you stuck in this imagined prison. All the restrictions you place on yourself because you fear you are not good enough, smart enough, wealthy enough, strong enough, pretty enough, etc., restricts your potential and keeps you locked up. The door to your mind-made prison has been unlocked the whole time. You created a list of reasons inside your mind as to why you should remain in confinement. You believe you are a bad person, you don't deserve, and you are unworthy. Recognize that the prison you created for yourself is unlocked and wide open, but it's your beliefs that make you think it's locked and that you cannot leave at your own free will. You must stop holding yourself a prisoner to self-doubt and false beliefs and step out of the mind-made prison you created for yourself. Think of it this way, the person who put you in prison is yourself, that person has the keys all you have to do is take the keys and step forward to release yourself from the prison you put yourself into.

The self-imposed limitations will be lifted freeing you from the chains of denial, lack, and burden. You are the only person that has the power to bring yourself the level of freedom and ease you desire. It's time to unshackle your emotional restraints by being kind to yourself, ceasing to judge yourself, dropping your ideal of perfectionism, and finally getting out of your own way. If you waited for things to be perfect before you act, you probably wouldn't get out of bed every day. You are not perfect, nobody is.

We put many restrictions on ourselves and come up with a multitude of reasons why we can't get this, can't have that, ever achieve this, never acquire that. This incessant inner doubt is nothing but crippling. It blocks progress and keeps us from taking risks. This leads to playing small and hiding our light and the unique gifts we have to share. To live our greatness we need to stop suppressing our inner gifts and awaken our gifts.

Love yourself unconditionally and give others the opportunity to do the same. Love the good parts, the bad parts, and the shadow parts. The shadow parts are the parts you hate and try to repress. Carl Jung coined the term "the shadows" and defined them as being the "unknown dark side of the personality." You try to hide the shadow parts. Debbie Ford writes about this in the *Dark Side of The Light Chasers*, "Our shadows hold the essence of who we are. They hold our most treasured gifts. By facing these aspects of ourselves, we become free to experience our glorious totality: the good and the bad, the dark and the light."

Make a commitment to love yourself through all your fears unconditionally. Learn to love yourself through the good and the bad. Don't let your past hold you back. You have already paid for your past mistakes. You are a human being, and it's okay to make mistakes. Let go of the persecution of the past. Use your missteps as opportunities to become a better version of yourself. Make it a goal to love yourself unconditionally. Know that you are enough. You are perfect as you are despite the mistakes you've made or the flaws you believe you have. Every day and every minute is a new opportunity to change your thoughts and change your life. Be gentle with yourself through your journey of healing the mind and body. The moment you consciously commit to feeling better to yourself and limiting contact with negative people and environments your life will become less complicated, and the road ahead will be smoother.

On occasion, you will feel drained, tired, unhealthy, uninspired, sad, unworthy or a number of other emotions. By being conscious of those challenging moments, you can get past them and get connected to your truth. When these moments arise, sit with your emotions and allow yourself to really feel them. Does it feel new? Is it an old hurt? When was the first time you can remember feeling this way? Where do you feel it in your body? Send love to that area. Thank the feeling for being there and aiding you along your journey through healing. Negative emotions are like whispers or little nudges pushing you to take action and change what is not working for you. Stop ignoring yourself and tend to yourself. If you choose to ignore the initial signals eventually, those little nudges will desperately try to get your attention and whispers will quickly escalate into screams, and the signals will also quickly escalate into things that are much harder to deal with. Tackle them when they are manageable, so it's easier to get passed them. As Carl Jung aptly noted, "What you resist persists." When you do heal the mind and body, you will tap into the universal flow and live the life you deserve.

11

PERCEPTION DECEPTION

"The eye sees only what the mind is prepared to comprehend."
– Robertson Davies

I t is part of human nature to interpret and judge surroundings, people, things, and situations we encounter in our lives. We are constantly assessing everything around us. Our perceptions are created from the interpretations, judgments, and the environment of what we are observing. You are who you perceive yourself to be in any given moment. If you judge someone to be confident and empowered, then you will perceive them as being confident and empowered unless you change your opinion about them. If you perceive yourself as being weak and timid, you will behave weak and timid until you believe otherwise.

Perception is infinitely changeable. However, our perceptions become fixed based on beliefs and can be deceiving. For example, If you perceive yourself as being flawed, when you look in a mirror you will be searching for flaws whether you have any or not. The more you look, the more things you will find to support your perceptions of whether flaws exist or not. You see what you perceive to be flawed and believe that's what everyone else sees as well. You were born into this world as a perfect creation, a whole, and complete human being. I spent years believing I had big ears until one day I looked in the mirror and decided they were too small. I became equally fixed on these two opposing beliefs at different times based on my perception at that moment. Your perception about yourself is distorted and is keeping you from seeing your wholeness. Left unchecked you will continue to look for reasons to deny your wholeness.

We have a tendency to label experiences and create meanings that are based on perception. If your friend forgot your birthday, would you be hurt, would you be infuriated, offended, or would you just let it slide? Everyone's interpretation of events is individual, and we judge experiences to mean something specific for us. Another individual can have the identical experience as you did, but each person will have a different perception of what happened, and therefore, will take away something different from the exchange based on individual perceptions.

My friend forgot my birthday once, and I was really hurt. I searched for why I took it so hard. I realized I was looking for external validation and put too much value in the opinions of others and the things they say or do. When a person forgets your birthday, it means whatever you decide it means. We can come up with a myriad of reasons why a person did or didn't do something. Or behave a certain way. I believed my friend didn't value me or love me and I made a big story around what it meant. Separate the made up drama in your mind from the actual truth. What actually transpired? Based on your beliefs you have ascribed meaning to why they forgot your birthday. If you can separate the truth from your perception, you will see that it's not as big a deal as you made it out to be. Your mold can have you believing all sorts of reasons, as to why a person acted as they did. Reasons like, "I'm not as important to them as they are to me. They don't love me because I'm unlovable. They don't care about me because I'm worthless. They hate me because I'm a bad person." or "They are breaking up with me because everyone abandons me."

Every day there is someone, somewhere celebrating a birthday. So, in the course of your lifetime, it's feasible that someone you know may forget to extend to you their birthday wishes. Most likely it will have nothing to do with you and has no meaning other than they forgot. If your spouse or significant other forgot your birthday you might have a different expectation of them; therefore the degree of your reaction may be significantly higher than if it was your friend or acquaintance who forgot your birthday. When your husband or boyfriend hasn't mentioned your birthday all day because clearly, they forgot you may have felt completely rejected or infuriated. Whereas, if your friend or co-worker forgot to wish you a happy birthday you might have been mildly upset.

Have you ever been offended by a voicemail message because you perceive the tone of the message as being unfriendly or rude? You may have listened to it a few more times to make sure it was as offensive as you thought. Now, you're sure it wasn't a friendly message, and you're really pissed off and decide the person who left the message is a total jerk. You're so annoyed you call a friend to complain about the message you received. Now you grow even madder as you continue to recount the message. You tell your friend on the phone what a terrible day you've had and the voicemail message seemed fitting to the type of day you had.

A few days go by, and you listened to the message again, and this time you don't hear a shred of unfriendliness or rudeness. In fact, you may even hear a pleasant tone in the message. So what happened? Your thoughts and feelings create your experience. The voicemail message never changed but your mood, while listening to it again, did change. When you look back, you realize you were in a bad mood and you were pissed off before you even listened to the message. You're mood dictated how you heard and interpreted the message. You judged the message based on how you were feeling and not on what was actually said. The next time you find yourself in a situation like this recognize that what is happening may be based on a false perception. Separate the facts from the perception that may be clouding your judgment.

I have been living in the same condo for a few years, and my custom made grey crushed velvet sofa was looking tattered and worn. It was sun-faded, and my favorite spot to sit was clearly worn out. I hadn't noticed the gradual decline in years, but when I noticed it, it was so obvious I wondered how I missed it. I obsessed about it for weeks. Do I buy a new sofa or do I get the cushions re-upholstered? One day, on the hunt for a missing USB stick I had to move the long seat cushion. The seat cushion was clipped into place in several spots. I unclipped the cushion, found the USB stick and then I flipped the cushion and secured it back into place. The weathered look of the cushion was erased in just one flip. I couldn't believe all I had to do was unclip the cushion and flip it. My sofa looked brand new again. What do you need to flip around in order to see improvement? What's on the flipside of your thinking? I looked at that sofa in amazement for several days. I marveled at how the sofa that had given me stress, in an instant makeover, looked brand new again. The solution was right in front of me the whole time. I wondered why it took me so long to flip it. Become a master at flipping your perceptions. An actor looks for the motivation behind a scene. My acting coach said when analyzing a scene and understanding the motivation behind it flip it around and do the opposite of what you think, and it will probably be right. If something is not working for you, consider that there is always another way of looking at the same thing and getting a different result. If you flip it around you just may have the perfect solution to your problem.

The lock on the front door of my condo was getting sticky. When I inserted the key, it would jam, and I would have to wiggle it back and forth a few times to shake it loose. It gradually grew worse, and it was a continuous struggle to get the key in and out, and I was afraid it was going to break in half. Then I'd be stuck having to pay for a locksmith. One day, I decided I was going to do something about it. I looked up how to fix a sticky lock on the Internet. The solution was so simple. Just one little squirt of lubricant oil and the awkward jagged motion when I inserted the key disappeared. I couldn't believe it was that easy. It made me wonder why I had put up with it for so long and what else I was putting up with that had an easy fix. Sometimes the ease of a fix comes from just wanting it to be fixed.

What are you struggling with and why are you putting up with it? What steps can you take to fix the situation? Maybe all you need is a new perspective? I needlessly struggled with the door lock every day for months, and yet the solution was always there. Rather than looking for the fix, I kept focusing on the problem. I found the solution when I was ready to perceive the problem from a new vantage point. The solution to your struggle is probably much easier than you think. View your struggles with a new perspective. Flip the obstacles that you are currently putting up with. Try imagining what your life would look like without the obstacles you are experiencing. When you visualize being free of challenges, you are no longer focusing on the problem, and it then becomes much easier to identify a solution because your mind is not preoccupied with the problem.

Your perception can be altered to shape and create your reality. At the suggestion of my naturopath, I was put on a Gluten free, dairy free diet and was given a whole list of other offending foods that I had to eliminate from my diet. I knew I needed an action plan if I was going to have any chance of sticking to this diet. I realized that the best way to get through this diet of perceived depravity was to not focus on all the foods I should avoid but rather focus on the foods I could enjoy that nourished my body. With a shift in my perception, I went from lacking food I wanted to an abundance of food that is healthier for me. Then, I found it relatively easy to eliminate the foods I previously thought were impossible to live without.

By focusing on a list of foods that are healthy and good for me, the sense of depravity I initially felt was replaced with a sense of well-being. The list of foods to avoid was no longer overwhelming. What experiences do you find overwhelming? What emotions are you having trouble digesting? How can you switch your perception and gain a new outlook so life can become more manageable? Don't give time to what is not working but rather focus on what is working for you. Find what is working in your life. When you alter your perception and stop focusing on what is wrong or missing your life will improve.

12

THE STRENGTH OF VULNERABILITY AND THE FUTILITY OF GUILT

"Vulnerability sounds like truth and feels like courage. Truth and courage aren't always comfortable, but they're never weakness."
— *Brené Brown*

Vulnerability is an essential part of being human. It allows you to be authentic, compassionate, and empathetic. It may be difficult for you to be vulnerable, particularly if you were raised to believe vulnerability is a sign of weakness. Vulnerability is not a weakness. It takes a tremendous amount of courage to be vulnerable, to put yourself out there, to express your feelings fully and be judged by others. If you avoid the circumstances and people in your life in order to avoid being vulnerable you miss the chance of sharing who you are at a deep core level and being honest, whole, and complete. Being vulnerable is an extraordinary gift you give yourself and those around you.

Being vulnerable and expressing emotion in front of others can be frightening and intimidating because you open yourself up to their judgment. Many believe vulnerability is a sign of weakness, in which case, the mere thought of expressing your feelings and exposing your vulnerabilities, even to yourself, can be downright terrifying. In sharing your feelings, you resurrect forgotten parts of yourself that lie deeply buried within you. The truth is the ability to be vulnerable and express it to others is a great strength. It is from your most exposed and raw moments that growth and real progress can be made.

When you are afraid to show your vulnerability you hide your emotions, you start to build a protective wall to prevent yourself from being hurt, and you lose connection to your core self. This wall you have built is extremely effective at keeping others from getting to close to you. However, it's also great at keeping you walled off from your potential. No one can get past your walls, but your greatness can't get out either because it is trapped within the barrier you created. When you break down your protective wall, you free all emotions and desires hidden inside. Being vulnerable and letting your guard down is a necessary and crucial step to living an authentic life.

The fear of being judged and looking like a failure is created from the anticipation of a negative response or unfavorable reaction from others. Rather than focusing on how others may respond or react when you express your vulnerability ask yourself what you can gain or learn from expressing your thoughts, feelings from your core being. You may have been vulnerable in the past and felt doing so didn't go as well as you would have wanted, you may have been left feeling awful and thought it was a complete mistake, in which case, this created a belief that you will feel this way every time you are authentic and share from your deepest core. Someone controlled by their limiting beliefs may not have it within themselves to act in a supportive, loving way towards you. Rather than taking it personally remember that their response is not about you but rather from their own fears and insecurities. What's important is that you took the chance to be you regardless of the outcome. You will make significant headway in the quality of your relationships and your life when you take a chance and express yourself, be open and step out and do that which gives you no guarantees. You will experience an expansion of your true self and gain confidence knowing you were able to step through your hesitations and fears.

When you do step past your hesitations and fears despite the uncertainty of the outcome your creativity and passions resurface. You no longer have to hide who you are or pretend to be who you are not. Vulnerability deepens your relationship with yourself and your connection to others. Vulnerability is always scary when you focus on what could go wrong when expressing your feelings. Rather than focusing on the worst that can happen when you show your vulnerable side, focus on the good that will come when you openly and honestly present yourself. You will be more authentic and true to who you really are, and as a result, you can have an open and honest exchange with others, rather than being closed in by your barriers. The fear of being vulnerable blocks out the truth of who we are. You must be honest and authentic to be at your best. It's time to tackle those fears and live authentically.

As children, we absorb everything around us and begin to define and shape our personalities by what we believe and what we have chosen to hold on to. Our childhoods are the birthplace of many insecurities and doubts. As adults, our life experiences have equipped us with adequate reasoning to quiet past doubt. Find the strength to be vulnerable, and you can silence your insecurities, which keep you focused on what others think and not on what you think. Embrace your vulnerability and discover a new facet of your being. As children, we do not have the same capacity to reason as adults; however, we can commit to making a choice as an adult to go back to the past and eradicate the limiting insecurities born from childhood beliefs and comfort our inner child that needs care and attention.

In order to appear as if you have it all together, you may pretend you don't show emotion and project an image that you are never hurt, never angry or never sad and avoid sharing yourself and exposing your vulnerability.

You believe you will avoid looking bad in front of others if you show no emotion, however, no one is impervious to emotion. Take the first step and let others know how you feel. Share your challenges and give someone the opportunity to just listen and really hear you. Be vulnerable so you can expose the real and authentic you. If you still don't feel safe sharing your story with anyone then write it down in a journal. When you commit the words to paper, you create an intention to free repressed emotion. The act of writing out your feelings can be a powerful healing tool.

Vulnerability is being present to your emotions and your feelings and being able to openly share them with others regardless of the expectation or outcome. Push yourself to be comfortable with being uncomfortable, get connected to your core and share your greatest challenges, deepest fears, insecurities, and most heartfelt desires and wishes and be wholly and completely you. Detach yourself from the outcome, show your strength, be vulnerable, and learn to express your feelings fully.

Guilt and Guilt Transfer

Guilt is like paying excess baggage fees even when you have no luggage. It is a futile emotion that always comes at a price. You are guilty for the things you say or do and guilty for the things you don't say or do. We can feel guilty for endless reasons and even take on guilt from others which doesn't belong to us.

In childhood, we are blamed and shamed for getting things wrong and told we are stupid and taught that we should be ashamed of ourselves. We are made to feel we are bad, inadequate, inferior and thus end up believing others are right, more important, worthy and deserving. You see when we've done something considered wrong we attribute it to mean that we are inherently wrong or bad as people as opposed to the action being wrong or bad. We then carry these insecurities and beliefs about ourselves through all areas of life and feel guilty for not being a better, smarter person.

Not only do we feel guilty about the things we did or didn't say or do, but we also run the risk of picking up other people's guilt. Because you feel inadequate, you take ownership of other people's guilt, shame or hurt and replace your feelings with theirs. You suppress your feelings and make other's feelings more important than your own because you don't think you're good enough for your feelings to even count. You also trade speaking up for yourself for guilt. An unfair trade made by the subconscious mind.

With a little bit of effort and intent on your part, you can let go of guilt or transferred guilt. First, cut yourself some slack and let go of any of your own guilt that you are carrying. Then, recognize some of the guilt you feel as your own is actually someone else's that you have chosen to carry with you. It's not yours and does not belong to you. Release it and then let go of any guilt or put upon guilt that you are carrying. You must remember that you were born perfect, whole and complete, without blame or shame, and that you don't need to carry guilt with you when you didn't deserve it.

13

NEGATIVE-NARRATIVE – THE INNER CRITIC

"The words you speak become the house you live in."
– Hafiz

Great thoughts can quickly turn bad when patterns of negative thinking infiltrate your mind. It has been said that we have between 50,000 to 70,000 thoughts per day, and it's estimated that approximately eighty percent of our daily thoughts are negative. Unfortunately, your mold is the primary contributor to the negative content of your daily thoughts. Did you know that you have, for the most part, the same thoughts every day? This means that yesterday's thoughts are influencing today's thoughts. If you leave negative thoughts unchecked, you run the risk of having the same negative pattern repeat over and over again.

You can stop the inner negative-narrative by first becoming aware of what you are thinking and then working to rid your mind of negative thoughts. Negativity sabotages your happiness with each destructive thought. Let's clean up the negative junk in your emotional house that does not serve you, and strengthen your emotional constitution.

One way to uncover your negative-narrative is to notice your thoughts when you are doing something new for the very first time. When you have already accomplished something, it brings certainty that you can do it again. However, when you are doing something you've never done before you have no history of success and therefore feel uncertain of the outcome. In this case, your insecurities can skyrocket because you haven't yet proven you can do it and success is not guaranteed. If you were to check in with your thoughts at these times of uncertainty, you would probably hear your negative-narrative screaming at you.

Years ago, I tried something new and attended a singing workshop. What I learned was far more than singing, the most valuable lesson I gained had, in fact, nothing to do with singing. In the moments before I would get up in front of the class to sing, I started to recognize the awful things that ran through my head while waiting my turn. Thoughts like, "I have no talent, I am a failure, I don't deserve to be here, everyone is more talented than me, I don't belong here, why did I bother coming? I should leave, I can't sing." On and on went the destruction of my self-esteem because of the negative-narrative. I was acutely aware I needed to break the pattern of thinking causing this overbearing dialogue. So, I began to challenge my thoughts. Why was I so tough on myself? Recognizing destructive thoughts is the first step in discovering your negative-narrative.

There is a direct correlation between the negative-narrative and your mold. Your mold is overloaded with all the negatives you believe about yourself. Your brain is constantly looking for ways to reaffirm your false beliefs and limitations. When you are experiencing any type of success or growth your mold is lurking in the background ready to challenge your success. When things are going well, your mold jumps in to challenge your new beliefs. You can stop the subconscious sabotage by refusing to believe the destructive thoughts. When you are experiencing difficult times in your life the discomfort and uncertainty that comes with challenges will bring out your insecurities. You may feel inadequate or somehow feel as if you are to blame for the difficulty. Insecurities can emerge as a negative voice in your head.

Your negative-narrative can also be triggered by memories. As you recall a past scenario, you attach an inner dialogue to accompany the memory. This negative dialogue makes it increasingly harder to see the memory in any light but negative. Rather than letting the thought pass, it plays a continuous loop in our minds. If you can recognize and interrupt the negative-narrative, you will stop the loop. Soon, you will find it easier to become aware of the daily negative thoughts and free yourself from old emotional debris. Then you'll start to remember times without the added negativity.

The things that you beat yourself up about can seem ridiculous to someone else but be very real to you. Ask yourself, would you be as hard on someone else as you are on yourself? Of course, you wouldn't. You probably wouldn't even be a fraction as hard on them as you are with yourself. If you have grown accustomed to beating yourself up, for real or perceived offenses, your reactions then become automatic. Given the right circumstance, you throw yourself under the bus without a second thought. Your stupid mold feeds off this negative-narrative and becomes increasingly powerful and destructive.

When you reject yourself, you are giving others the opportunity to reject you. When you reject yourself, you block your inner light and press the pause button on happiness. You are hiding from yourself and blocking the good that wants to come to you. To quiet the negative-narrative write 10 things you love and appreciate about yourself. If you can't think of anything that you love about yourself, then list some qualities that you dislike in others. Then write out the complete opposite of the negative qualities. Study the positive list and choose the qualities that make you feel good. Write those qualities down on a new sheet of paper and use this as your list of what you love about yourself. Read the list every day. Carry your list with you. Whenever you find yourself thinking negative thoughts about yourself, then take the list out and read it. As you read the things you love about yourself, let the words sink in.

The following exercise is a way for you to turn down the volume on your negative-narrative instantly. Anytime you notice your negative-narrative stop and envision a radio volume dial in your mind's eye. See the numbers 0 through 10 on the dial with 10 indicating the maximum volume level. Set the dial to 10. The number 10 is base set-point for your self-talk. The loud and obtrusive self-talk in your mind that incessantly plays on repeat. Let the words of your negative-narrative be blaring and annoying. When the sound feels uncomfortably loud begin to turn down the volume. When you are aware of your negative-narrative, I want you to turn down the volume from 10. Move the dial down gradually down from 9-8-7. With every turn of the dial hear the words gradually getting quieter and more distant. When the volume dial numbers go down your negative-narrative gets quieter, and along with that, the negative-narrative begins to lose its impact and meaning. Continue to turn down the volume from 6-5-4 and again feel the thoughts losing substance. Then again, turn the dial down from 3-2-1. The negative-narrative is diminishing and losing strength as you turn down to each level. At volume 1 the sound is so low you can barely hear. Now, turn down the volume to 0 and completely mute your negative-narrative dialogue until the negative voice no longer exists or holds any meaning. You have now turned down the volume of your inner critic.

Remember, we have mostly the same thoughts every day. When you continue to quiet negative thoughts, they will no longer play over and over, day in and day out. With this exercise, you will be able to recognize your negative thoughts and dismiss them by dialing down the volume from 10 to zero. This allows you to create something new in its place. It's an open canvas for you to design a future you are excited about. You will transform negative thoughts, stop the negative-narrative that relentlessly plays on repeat and create a positive narrative that supports your life and your dreams. Dial down the negative-narrative and silence your inner critic. Step out of the negative emotional house. Give yourself a break! You deserve it!

14

IDENTIFYING AND BREAKING YOUR STUPID MOLD

*"The only limit to our realization of
tomorrow will be our doubts of today."*
– Franklin D. Roosevelt

W e all have "go-to" words or phrases that
we often repeat or use to punctuate a
sentence. Words like absolutely, really,
whatever, awesome, or phrases like "I love that," "It is
what it is," "I see," "You know what I mean?" When
you stop to consider the words you repeat on a daily
basis, you can identify your "go to" words or phrases.
Similarly, we also have words or phrases that we use
to emotionally sabotage ourselves or put ourselves
down. Those words, phrases or thoughts are not as
easily identifiable because they are deeply buried in

the subconscious. These words or phrases become how we define and shape our personalities, creating a false identity, until we realize what we are saying to ourselves and we decide to stop and break the cycle of verbal self-destruction.

You must work to uncover the destructive language you are using. What are your "negative go-to" phrases? Keep a journal and write down the words or phrases that you use throughout the day to sabotage yourself. Look at what you wrote down and circle any repetitive words or phrases. Notice the words that stand out the most for you when you are hard on yourself. Find the words that have power over you. Do you tell yourself you are stupid, an idiot, a loser, unworthy, useless, a failure, never good enough? It's important to note here that there are key memories from childhood that played a paramount role in shaping your identity and self-worth or rather lack of self-worth. These memories often play over and over in our minds like scenes from an old movie. If you discover these bring forth negative feelings, then it is time to admit the recurring themes have played out for way too long in your life and that you can press the stop button now.

Sometimes it is helpful to look at your family members or close friends that you see on a regular basis. They act as your mirror and reflect back your thoughts and beliefs. It is much easier to identify actions and behaviors in others. If you have grown up in the same household as your siblings or parents it is likely you have similar thoughts and beliefs, and ways that you critique or admonish yourself. You may have a family member who always needs to be right, is controlling, has low self-esteem and incessantly belittles themselves or is an outright bully. Make a list of the negative and positive behavioral patterns you see in them. Honestly, ask yourself if you share any of these same behaviors.

Pay extra attention to the behaviors you dislike or even hate in others because, often times, what you despise in them you share in common with them. For example, if you can't stand a work colleague or business associate because they incessantly talk about themselves or put others down, take a look at yourself and see if you do the same. You may be surprised to find you have the same negative behavior.

You may have had unrealistic expectations of yourself when you were a child and unnecessarily carried those expectations into adulthood. This may be caused by the belief that you are stupid or not good enough. No matter what you say or do your actions are never enough or you feel stupid, so you try to compensate by trying to know everything and when you don't know everything you are "stupid," as your false identity suggests.

One way to help break the cycle of demanding too much of yourself and then putting yourself down for not achieving your expectations is to observe the children around you. Watch how young kids interact and behave with others. As you watch the children around you, listen to the vocabulary and notice how they behave.

What expectations did you have for them in contrast to the kind of expectations you had for yourself? I caution you to be mindful when observing your own children because you may have unwittingly passed on those same unrealistic expectations and may not be objective in your observation. I had an aha moment when I was aware of the interaction between my nieces and nephew when they were younger. I realized the expectations I had of myself at their age were absolutely impossible to reach. It was probably unrealistic for an adult to obtain let alone a child or a teenager.

Children have a lifetime of lessons and learning ahead of them which would shape them into being. They need continual guidance. There is no way they could or should have things figured out. Seeing the innocence in my nieces and nephew, I recognized that I was blind to my own innocence. As a young teenager, I thought I should know everything and have it all figured out. As an adult, I understand figuring it out is a lifelong process. Why could I not see that innocence in myself? We are not designed to know everything. We gain knowledge through our self-evolution and life experiences. The contrast here is between what is expected and demanded of ourselves to what children are mentally or physically capable of achieving given their age. For example, it is not possible for a child to get a driver's license given their age. No matter how much effort is put in it is not obtainable.

This is how we go through life. Striving for the

unobtainable and making ourselves wrong for not achieving it. Another option to break the cycle is to remember, as you were growing up, the children around you. How did those children interact and behave with you and others? As you see your memory of the children around you, do you recall what you did or said? Try to recall and identify any contrast in what you demanded of yourself. Was it acceptable for others to guess the wrong answers but when you said the wrong answer you believed you should have known better and were an idiot because you got it wrong? Were you encouraging to others when they didn't get things right on a first try but when you weren't successful at a first attempt you believed you could never do anything right? Was it acceptable for others to miss a goal when playing a game but you were a loser when you didn't score and should have tried harder? Identifying past situations when you demanded the obtainable for yourself can help you identify other areas in life where your expectations are unrealistic or unobtainable.

When you deem others to be good, honest or kind and they disappoint you and fall short of your expectations, you're left to question your judgment. You wonder how you could have been so wrong about someone. You doubt your intuition and decisions. It may be valid to question your judgment, but it is not fair to punish yourself for getting things wrong. This is completely unnecessary and counterintuitive. Whether you were deceived or not by the other person doesn't matter. You made a mistake. People show you what they want you to see and you base your assessment on their projection, not their personality. You made an assessment based on what they chose for you to see at that moment, and that was what you had to work with at the time. Behaviors and attitudes can shift at any given time. An individual can project different behaviors with different people in different settings. You would naturally define their behavior on your personal interaction with them while others would do the same. Therefore, you may have completely different conclusions about the same person. Whether you are right or wrong is irrelevant. What is important is that you stop beating yourself up for believing you were a bad judge of character. Things happen, people change or deceive us and sometimes we just get it wrong. I judged from a quick glance at a stranger who was well groomed and neatly dressed, in an underground parking lot to be harmless and I got it wrong. I thought he was heading for the elevators, but he was looking for a place to hide near the elevators. He was dangerous, and there is no way I could have known that at first glance.

I kept thinking that I must be a bad judge of character. I began to second guess all my decisions. I asked myself over and over how could I be so wrong. Then I told myself I made the best decision for what I thought was the situation. You must come to terms with and accept everything that has happened in your life so you can be free to move forward without limiting blocks. When you live authentically in the present, the past no longer defines you and greatness will become your future. I want you to be committed to valuing yourself no matter what difficulties you are going through. I want to show you that you have the ability to release old worn out thoughts, patterns, habits, and beliefs and to choose to live an abundant, happy, and fulfilled life. Find what's inside your stupid mold and break the limiting beliefs you shaped and formed like softened clay molded that solidified and hardened over time trapping you into a false identity.

The first step to breaking your stupid mold is to find out what's inside. So, think of the words you use when you are critical of yourself. What do you say to yourself when you make a mistake or say the wrong thing? Notice the words you use to admonish yourself when you believe you've done something wrong or when you are self-critical? What words stand out and wield power over you? Do you tell yourself that you are stupid or not enough? Have you deemed yourself to be an idiot, a loser, unworthy, useless? Pick the words that have the most impact. Feel the emotion behind the words. Be completely honest with yourself. Don't force the words. Let the words reveal themselves to you. Feel the emotion connected to each word. Do not judge, simply feel and observe.

When you identify the words that resonate the strongest, you will discover the limiting beliefs that have been controlling your life. These words are the key to your limiting beliefs. The following meditation is designed to help you uncover words buried in your subconscious that you are unaware of so you can break your limiting patterns and regain your power.

Meditation for Overcoming Limiting Beliefs

You can listen to this guided meditation online at
www.taniakolar.com.

Find a comfortable spot either sitting or lying down. When you are comfortable, close your eyes and take a long deep breath in through the nose and slowly exhale out through the nose. Take another deep breath in through the nose and slowly exhale out through the nose. On the next breath in through the nose deeply inhale and fully exhale out through the nose releasing any tension in the body. Feel your body becoming more and more relaxed with each exhalation. Repeat one more time, slowly inhale through the nose and on the next exhale out through the nose allow your body to relax even deeper. Now, let your breathing return to a natural rhythm.

Imagine you are in the middle of a beautiful garden. What does your garden look like? Are you surrounded by lush trees, healthy greenery, and brightly colored flowers? Is there a pond with water lilies and koi fish? Can you smell the fragrant flowers or the crisp, fresh air? Do you hear the sound of birds chirping or the sound of babbling water? Feel the calmness and tranquility as you take in the serenity and beauty around you. You feel relaxed and at peace. Now you see a path, the path leads to a large wooden door with an antique brass doorknob. Make your way onto the path and walk towards the door. This door is a gateway to your past.

On the other side of the door is your younger self. You are going to step back in time as a guardian to your younger self. In a moment, and on the count of three, you will open the door and see a younger you at a time when you felt like you were unworthy or unlovable. Go back to the earliest memory you can remember. Perhaps it was a time when you felt bad or guilty for doing something wrong, or when you felt like a failure. On the count of three, you are going to turn the doorknob, open the door and step into your past. One, two, three, you are now back in time at a moment when you felt unlovable and unworthy. There before you is your younger self. In this memory how old are you? Look around and see who else is there and what everyone is doing. Observe your younger self as they experience the memory. How does your younger self feel? Do they feel sad, guilty, worthless or unlovable? What are they saying or thinking to themselves? Are they saying they are a failure, ugly, stupid, or bad? What do they believe about themselves? Do they think they always make mistakes and can't do anything right? Do they feel shame? Do they believe they can't have what they want because they don't deserve it? What beliefs have they taken on as their own, did someone tell them they were useless, a loser or will never amount to anything?

Go up to your younger self, your inner child. Tell them everything is going to be alright, that you are here now. Comfort your inner child's feelings of sadness, unworthiness, anger, guilt, shame, hatred, resentment or whatever they are feeling right now. Wrap your arms around them and tell them it's okay and you understand if they felt they were bad, or felt guilty, like a failure or not good enough. Tell your younger self it's not their fault and they are worthy and lovable and perfect just as they are. Tell them to forget all the negative things people said and all the bad things they believe about themselves. Those are past beliefs that aren't needed anymore. Tell them to let go of any fears and trust that this is just a memory of their past. All the negative things they were told or believed about themselves are not true. They are perfect no matter what happened in the past. Tell your younger self you are their guardian and will always love and protect them. Look your younger self in the eyes with unconditional love and understanding. Give your younger self a big hug and say you love them.

It's time to leave the past behind and step into the future they love and deserve. In a moment, you are going to walk together through the gateway to the future. Take your younger self by the hand and as their guardian promise them you are going to take care of them. All the negative thoughts and limiting beliefs they have, no longer have meaning in the future. On behalf of your inner child repeat after me: "I am no longer defined by the limitations of my past. I am ready to step into my future and live an extraordinary life of greatness. I am loveable. I am worthy. I am enough. I deserve. I am limitless. I am greatness."

Now, make your way towards the large wooden door, the gateway to your future. On the count of three, turn the doorknob, open the door and step into your future. When you step through the door the past as you know it will no longer exist. One, two, three, now step into your future. As you pass through to the other side of the door into your future, your inner child merges and becomes one with you. You have cleared the past and made space for new experiences and new beliefs for you and your inner child who will forever be a loving part of you.

In the near distance, you see a garden. It seems comforting and familiar. This is your ideal garden that you designed exactly as you wanted it. Now you are going to design the future you want. What are your most heartfelt desires? What future do you want for yourself? Design it in your mind's eye. See it and feel it as though it is already yours. You are liberated from your past conditioning and have regained complete control of your future. There is nothing holding you back from the life you desire. Stand tall and feel empowered. You have created a clear space where you can stand in your greatness unhindered by limitations from your past. This space has no limitations and is full of endless possibility. It's a space where you are free to be yourself and create anything you want. Feel the energy in your entire body becoming alive with a new sense of purpose and passion. On the count of three, you will gently open your eyes. When you open your eyes you will feel incredibly relaxed, centered and have a strong knowing that you are the creator of your life and can be, do, have, and achieve anything you want. One, two, three, now slowly open your eyes.

Congratulations, you have now identified and broken the stupid mold filled with limiting beliefs from your past. You have taken back control. The limiting beliefs that have been controlling your life no longer have power, meaning or significance. By breaking from your false self, you have created a whole new world of possibilities and can now claim the life of greatness that was destined for you. You are limitless potential. This is the beginning of new possibilities and an extraordinary life.

15

THE POWER OF FORGIVENESS

"Forgiveness is the fragrance the violet
sheds on the heel that has crushed it."
– Mark Twain

Developing a capacity to forgive people who hurt you is one of the most powerful things you can do to regain your happiness. Forgiveness is not easy, particularly if you have suffered trauma at the hands of another. However, forgiveness is necessary for the overall good of your well-being. It is essential to forgive and stop hurting over the mistakes made by others so that you can be at peace.

It's a waste of precious time constantly finding fault with people or circumstances. Forgiveness stops the inner turmoil caused by holding on to grudges, thoughts of hate, and of contempt. These negative thoughts accumulate and are compounded leaving you to pay the price of not letting go. This price comes at the expense of your happiness. You've already lived through your pain and by holding on to unloving thoughts you are prolonging the painful experiences of your past and unnecessarily adding to your unhappiness.

Forgiveness transforms unloving thoughts and dissolves the negative feelings and energy you've harbored towards someone for no matter how long. If you choose forgiveness, you will rid yourself of the emotional debt and the heavy burden you carry of accumulated negativity. Be careful not to overwhelm yourself in this process. Take small steps when you are ready keeping in mind doing so will bring you closer to being free of emotional hardship. We all have wounds, from wrongs committed in the past against us or that we have committed against others, and scars that run deep. There is no one who is without fault. We all have made plenty of mistakes, and we will continue to do so. I invite you to recognize and acknowledge the fact that we are not perfect and sometimes we are going to mess up. It is part of human nature to make mistakes, it is from our mistakes that we learn and grow. You will be less inclined to hate others when you accept that mistakes are universal.

There will come a time when you need to forgive others and a time when it is you who needs to be forgiven. There will be some bumps along your journey. You need to trust your struggle and know you are exactly where you are meant to be right now. Stand in your power, forgive and let go of your resentments. You can never be genuinely happy if you cannot renounce others or yourself for mistakes made. Let go of any hatred or anger you are carrying. Instead of persecuting someone for their mistakes or yourself for that matter, use those mistakes as opportunities to learn from and do better and be better. Put the broken parts of you together like a puzzle and reconstruct your wholeness. Start to build yourself up piece by piece by making peace with yourself and others.

In order to gain a better understanding of what forgiveness is, let's first look at what forgiveness is not. Forgiveness is not denying, avoiding or hiding your feelings, justifying actions, accepting blame or trying to change the past. It is not giving in or giving up, and it doesn't mean you have to invite the person who hurt you back into your life unless you want to. Forgiveness is not a weakness. It's not wishing whatever happened, never happened and it certainly doesn't mean you weren't adversely affected, victimized or traumatized by what transpired. In addition, forgiveness is not about making the other person feel better. Another person's feelings should never be your motivation in forgiveness.

So, what is forgiveness? Forgiveness is allowing love to replace the negativity that affects your life. It's acknowledging your anger and then letting it go, so it stops negatively impacting your life. You don't have to be friends with or engage in any kind of communication with the person who broke your trust. You don't have to trust them or even like them. Ultimately, forgiveness is a gift you give yourself. When you are so angry, you feel like you could harm someone it's impossible to choose forgiveness. You need to work backward and diffuse the intense emotion you are feeling. Find the pathway between hatred and forgiveness and work in small steps to go from where you are to where forgiveness is on that path. Forgiveness can be a long, tough process but when you commit to the choice of adopting a forgiving heart, the process will be shorter and easier for you.

Forgiveness requires that you be honest with yourself. Pretending you have forgiven someone or convincing yourself you have when in your heart you know you haven't is not forgiveness. In this case, you are in denial and hiding what you are feeling, rather than acknowledging, confronting and moving through your emotions. Forgiveness is a process with progressive and identifiable stages. I will describe the four stages that I consider to be the most effective. It's best to go through each of these stages when you feel completely ready. The stages do not have to be done all at once, nor do they have to be done alone, you may share your experience with a trusted friend or a professional counselor.

Stage One

You must acknowledge your hurt and feel your pain

You must acknowledge your hurt and feel your pain in order to take away your pain. Your raw and vulnerable feelings are comparable to a wound. A scab forms to protect the wound and allows the underlying skin cells to heal. If you pick off the scab, the wound is left exposed and vulnerable to further injury. Forgiveness is allowing your wounds to heal under the scab.

Whatever happened in one moment of time, which left

you devastated for many moments of time doesn't have to destroy you if you choose forgiveness. You are more resilient and powerful than you realize. You have the power within you to forgive all the people who hurt you, broke your trust or wronged you in any way. Forgiveness will restore love and bring you a level of happiness and freedom that's impossible to achieve if you avoid your hurt and pain.

It is paramount that you give yourself the opportunity to heal and stop making the wounds of the past deeper. It may take some time to heal the pains, but you must choose to forgive in order to feel better. When you move forward with a forgiving heart, you will discover that by genuinely forgiving even one person, you will naturally be more compassionate towards others, including yourself. Every moment is a new opportunity for you to make a better choice for the sake of your happiness. Again, you are not trying to pretend an event never happened; you are trying to find a new way of looking at it in order to regain happiness. Now you can move forward knowing you can put an end to your suffering and replace non-forgiveness with an inner peace that has been missing.

Stage Two

Relive and Understand

To relive the moment is not just to recall the moment but to be in the moment. See it and sense it. Go back and relive the moment. By first reliving the moment, you can then reflect on what transpired and what the challenges presented. Ask yourself these questions. Can you see the benefit in your challenge? Do you want to be happy? Do you want to stop suffering? Do you want inner peace? If you answered NO to any of the questions, or hesitated, then you are undeservedly hurting yourself. Ask yourself the questions again and notice what you are thinking and feeling. What are you saying to yourself? What emotions are coming up? Are you refusing to let go of your pain because of a limiting belief? Discover what is preventing you from choosing forgiveness.

Reliving the moments experienced when you were younger is a positive step towards forgiveness in that doing so allows you, now as an adult, to see more broadly both what happened and what challenges were posed. Give yourself time to heal as you relive these moments, and time to make sense of the thoughts and feelings that surfaced.

Stage Three

Imaging your Life

You can work it out by imaging what your life would be like if you gave up your resentments and anger. What would it look like and feel like if you could forgive? Imagine regaining your mental clarity, feeling unburdened, lighter, freer, and happier. It is hard when you have been betrayed, lied to, deceived, taken advantage of, cheated, abused, abandoned, manipulated, repressed, denied love, belittled, made to feel unworthy, undeserving or unlovable. Although you cannot change what has happened, you can change the meaning you've attributed to what transpired. When you can change the meaning, you can then give up your anger and resentment from the past.

Stage Four

Release the Anger and Resentment

Problems will arise when you can't release the anger and resentment, no matter how much time has passed. Holding on to non-forgiveness is misdirecting your energy to something that does not serve you. If you've thought about wanting to hurt or punish the other person, you're only punishing yourself in the process. Your mental clarity is lost when your focus is on anger or resentment. The person who hurt you may not be giving you a second thought, and yet you can't seem to stop thinking about them. Your thoughts and feelings are not being telepathically communicated, so in all likelihood, they have no idea what you are thinking or feeling. They may not even be alive, in which case, they can never know how you are feeling. You are the one living with your anger. Whatever issue you are dealing with has happened in the past, and you need to shift your thinking and make a concerted effort to give up your anger and resentment. Then thoughts of retaliation and contempt are replaced by inner peace.

The process of forgiveness may be slow, and that's

ok. It's worth the effort no matter how long it takes to renounce past transgressions. You can forgive anyone despite how horrible their actions were. Forgiveness is important to your personal well-being, not the person who needs to be forgiven. Holding on to a grudge or refusing to forgive someone is a form of self-abuse. Resentment is a block to love and happiness, and it's poisoning your heart, mind, and soul. Take all the time you need to become aware of your feelings and then let go of ill feelings toward others. Don't get distracted with thoughts of how you are going to forgive. Start with the intent to forgive and the rest will fall into place.

Resentment is giving others power over your emotions. You own that power, and you can take it back. There is no action required from others in order for you to forgive someone. They don't need to apologize, take responsibility, admit to what they did wrong or deserve your pardon. Forgiveness is for you. It's an act of self-love. Give yourself the gift of self-love. Love yourself by softening your heart, choosing forgiveness and allowing love and happiness back into your life. At the core of all forgiveness is the willingness to improve your current emotional state. You will dissolve anger and resentment and infinitely improve your happiness and overall well-being. Forgiving someone of their injustice doesn't make what they did right. What it does mean is you no longer wish to feed the negative thoughts that keep you tied to hurtful experiences in the past as if they just happened yesterday. Choose to move forward knowing that forgiveness will lighten the burden you carry. It's time to take care of you.

You may never get the validation or apology you seek however you can stop adding to your suffering and start paying off your emotional arrears by forgiving those who caused you physical, mental, or emotional anguish. Be wise enough to know that people make mistakes, and be brave enough to take your power back. If you don't take your power back and forgive the person you are upset with, they will continue to own your power and wield their power over your emotions and ultimately over you.

Clinical psychologist, Everett L. Worthington Jr., a prominent researcher in the area of forgiveness says there are two types of forgiveness, "Decisional Forgiveness" which involves deciding to forgive and letting go of angry and resentful thoughts toward the person who wronged you. "Emotional Forgiveness" involves replacing the negative emotions with positive feelings like compassion, sympathy, and empathy. www.evworthington-forgivenss. com.

One of the things that keep us from deciding to forgive is the need to find answers to why things happened in the first place. I caution you to avoid getting stuck looking for answers because you may never find one. The truth is you don't need to know the reason why things happened in order to forgive. Maintaining your resentments, anger and hatred develops into what I call recurring victimhood - a constant negative state of mind that controls you. Feeling compassion for others is a way to step out of your victimhood. When you start to feel compassion for others you will naturally be more compassionate towards yourself, your mistakes, your shortcomings, and your feelings. Healing comes by reframing your thinking. Whatever your challenges are, discover the value in reframing your thinking, and your challenges will start to disappear.

Holding on to non-forgiveness is letting bitterness, contempt, and revenge control your thoughts which in turn alters your entire existence. When you allow negative thoughts to dominate your life, you see everything as negative. It becomes habitual to focus only on negativity, and you unwittingly invite more of the same into your life. Even in a positive environment, you will create a negative experience based on your negative outlook. You choose to see what you want and turn your reality into that vision. One way to release your resentments is to write them down. Here is an exercise to help you get started.

"I Forgive You" Exercise

On one piece of paper write the words, "I am angry or upset with" and take a few minutes to think about people that you need to forgive. Then write down the first names that come to mind and add yourself. The most important person you can ever forgive is yourself. Ironically, you can also be the hardest person to forgive.

On a second piece of paper write "I am angry or upset with you because" and take a few minutes to think about why you're upset. What resentments are you carrying toward them? Write down any thoughts that come to mind. Do not question what comes to mind, just write. Don't worry about it looking pretty or perfect. Just put down anything that comes up for you. Get real with your feelings toward each person on your list. You can't forgive someone if you are not honest about what you are feeling.

Once you are finished writing all the names and reasons you are angry or upset, on a third piece of paper write the words "I forgive you" with the name of the person you forgive before the word "I." Now you are going to transfer what you wrote on the second piece of paper onto this third piece of paper. When you have finished transferring each point at the end write "Thank you" followed by their name, and the following sentence "I am freer, lighter and happier now that I choose to forgive you." When you are finished, read what you wrote out loud as though you were reading it to the person you are writing about. Then tear up the paper and throw it away.

This exercise can bring on intense emotions to surface as you release repressed memories and feelings that were suppressed deep in the subconscious. Don't judge your emotions just let yourself experience them. Repeat the process for each name on the first piece of paper. Work at your own pace and be gentle with yourself as you process what you are feeling. Forgiveness is a way for you to feel exponentially better and release the heavy burden you carry.

Make it your goal to heal your hurts and to go through

the stages of forgiveness to make a complete recovery. Resolve now, to be honest with yourself about your feelings towards others and yourself. Learn to transcend your negativity, hatred, and anger, stop blaming others or conjuring up reasons why you can't or shouldn't forgive someone. You can free yourself from the self-harm that comes from holding on to anger and resentment.

As you are learning to release feelings, be kind to yourself and never punish yourself for not being able to forgive. It is never too late to forgive others, even if they have passed on. Forgive past transgressions with an open and genuine heart so you can heal your pain and be at peace. Healing comes from your acceptance and willingness to let forgiveness in and leads you to the path of living your best life. The capacity to forgive all, including yourself is within you.

16

AFFIRMITUDE: AN AFFIRMATION WITH AN ATTITUDE OF GRATITUDE

"Gratitude makes sense of our past, brings peace for today, and creates a vision for tomorrow."
– Melody Beattie

Practicing gratitude every day and using affirmations has been widely accepted as a way of increasing higher consciousness and personal well-being. An expanded awareness leads to prosperity in all areas of your life.

Gratitude and affirmations individually are very powerful, but when you combine the power of gratitude with the declaration of affirmations, the effects are exponentially amplified. You invite more positivity, happiness, love, health, and abundance to enter into your life. I have created what I call an *affirmitude* which is an affirmation with an attitude of gratitude that can be used any time you want to expand your awareness and well-being. You can use an affirmitude any time you would normally express gratitude or say an affirmation. First, let's take a look at gratitude and affirmations individually and then I'll show you how to put them together to turbocharge the results.

Gratitude is being thankful for all that has shown up in your life, the people, things, opportunities, experiences and yes, even the setbacks. It is a way to appreciate the big and little things and also to deepen your relationships with the people in your life. Practicing gratitude each day allows you to notice and reflect on the many blessings you have.

One way to appreciate your blessings is to write them down in a journal. Make it a daily ritual to spend five minutes writing down all the things in your life, large and small, that you are grateful for: the personal victories, the insights, the moments, the achievements, just write everything down that you're grateful for. Daily gratitude journaling will help you adjust your focus and train your mind to look for more things to be grateful for. Your mind will constantly be searching for things to be thankful for and you will start to notice things that normally would go unnoticed and unacknowledged.

Another way to express gratitude is to create a *Gratitude Box*. A gratitude box is a plain cardboard box or a decorative box that has inside a collection of various items that represent what you are grateful for. Fill it with absolutely anything that makes you feel thankful. You can add pictures of the people or things that you love, cards, meaningful notes or love letters. You can write down favorite quotes, affirmitudes, compliments or the funny things people said that made you laugh. Tuck them away in your gratitude box so you can encapsulate the good feelings associated with each compliment you've received or anything that makes you feel good. On days when you are having a difficult time open your gratitude box, and go through the items you've placed inside. It's like a gift that you can open any time and give to yourself. I can guarantee it will shift your feelings in no time because when you go back and review the contents, you can't help but feel uplifted and grateful.

One more way to express gratitude is to write a *Love Me Letter*, a heartfelt note to yourself with all the things you appreciate about yourself. You can thank yourself for being a supportive friend; donating your time to a good cause; being there to pick up the pieces when your kids are struggling; being the designated driver; smiling at a stranger in the elevator; letting your other half watch the game when your favorite show was on; doing the dishes before bed when you were exhausted; having the courage to start a new hobby or career; challenging yourself in any way or thank yourself for being uniquely you and a remarkable human being. When you are finished writing the reasons you appreciate yourself and are grateful to be you, sign off with the words, "love me," and sign your name.

It can be challenging to be grateful when you are

experiencing times of hardship, loss, betrayal or misfortune. It is in these trying times that gratitude is the most useful. Don't hesitate to reach out to someone to express your appreciation. There is a myriad of ways to communicate now either electronically or the old-fashioned way of sending a card or letter.

If you find yourself being ungrateful at any time, you must shift your focus to one of thankfulness. You can be grateful for something that happened in the past or for the opportunities that are yet to appear. Being grateful for the things you desire that haven't shown up yet is a good way to manifest them into existence. You are creating a positive field of energy when you are in a state of gratitude. This is an ideal frequency to set your intentions and desires.

Many have wondered at some point who and how many would show up at their funeral when they die. Well, it honestly doesn't matter because you won't be there to find out, and it certainly won't bring you back. What does matter is that you show up as your best self in the life you are leading now. Be present to the now and each moment. Who can you be today? What can you do? Who can you show up for? Who can you love? Who can you inspire? Make the life you are living more meaningful. You won't be left to wonder who will show up at your funeral when you know you have shown up and given your best self in this life to everyone around you. The positive impact you can have in other's lives is just one more reason to be grateful. You won't need to wait until you are dead to know you were loved or made an impact on others.

There are endless things to be grateful for each and every day, including the contribution you bring to others, the actions you have taken, support or advice you were given, coaching you received, your talents or any skills you have acquired. Give thanks to strangers who smiled at you in the elevator or wished you a good day. Ask yourself who or what you are grateful for showing up in your life. Whose words touched you or inspired you? Or, you can be grateful for your commitment to others. Whose life did you undeniably impact?

If you can't find anything to be grateful for you can use the

G

R

A

T

I

T

U

D

E

List on the next page with a few things to get you going.

Generosity: *to give to others with an open heart without expecting anything in return.*

Resiliency: *the ability to bounce back and recover from any challenges I face.*

Ambition: *the earnest drive and determination that helps me attain my goals.*

Truth: *the opportunity to authentically express myself to others.*

Intuition: *the inspired guidance I receive which aids in my growth.*

Time: *the moments I spend with the people I love.*

Unconditional Love: *to love regardless of circumstances and without conditions or limits.*

Desire: *the strong longing I have for all the things I crave in life.*

Emotion: *the ability to be in touch with my feelings.*

Be thankful for where you are right now and see how far you have come. There may be times you believe you've had no progress or have taken a few steps backward in reaching your goals and desires, however, if you take a closer look you will see you have made positive headway in at least one area of your life if not all. Progression doesn't have to be monumental. The smaller incremental successes can be equally gratifying.

Affirmations are statements you consciously declare by word or thought to influence your future. They are normally positive but can come in other forms. By using affirmations, you are sending positive or negative thoughts and intentions to the Universe. You may be already using affirmations, without being aware you are, but you may be using them negatively. For instance, if you are concerned about a mistake you made if you say "I'm an idiot" you are negatively affirming that you think you are an idiot, but if you say "I will get through this" this is a positive affirmation to state your ability to move forward. Become aware of the type of affirmations you are currently saying and make sure your affirmations are not working against you.

It's easier to practice gratitude and be thankful or affirm what you desire when things are going well. However, it is important to find something to be grateful for even in the dark times when things are not going so well or not working out the way you intended. For example, I was told by one of the police officers assigned to my case that my attack couldn't possibly get any worse unless my attacker had a weapon. In a dark situation, I found myself being extremely grateful he didn't have a weapon. I fully understood the attack would have had a very different outcome if a weapon was involved. I am grateful it wasn't worse than it was. I created the following affirmitude to express gratitude and affirm feeling protected.

I recognize and acknowledge my blessings in unfavorable circumstance. Thank you, Universe, for protecting me from malevolent energies. I am overflowing with divine protection and gratitude now.

Affirmitudes are the amalgamation of gratitude and affirmations. It can improve all areas of your life, and it can make you feel more optimistic about your future. Merging affirmations with gratitude compounds the effects of each. In a state of stress, it can be difficult to clearly define what you are grateful for or what you want to affirm for yourself. It is in these very moments that practicing affirmitudes is even more crucial to your state of mind and wellbeing. It can melt away tension and stress and replace it with thoughts of hopefulness and acceptance.

No matter what circumstances you may face or find yourself in there is always something to be grateful for. Whenever you affirm what it is that you want and then add an attitude of gratitude to the statement you are creating an affirmitude. It doesn't matter if what you are grateful for is big or small. What matters is being consistent and committed to your affirmitudes.

I encourage you to use affirmitudes every day not only to feel appreciation, and set an intention for your day, but to transform your life. You can keep a list of your favorite affirmitudes with you where you can see the list every day. You can use affirmitudes when you are feeling down or having a bad day or when you're feeling ungrateful. Reciting an affirmitude can immediately shift your mood and make you happier or feel more gratitude.

Affirmitudes are a good way of redirecting your thoughts and reconditioning the mind. When you use an affirmitude, you are affirming what you want to experience or eliminate from your life. This brings you closer to knowing and living your truth. As a suggestion greet each morning and end each night with an affirmitude or say them throughout the day. Be grateful for everything that has or hasn't shown up in your life, and declare with conviction what you want for yourself. Set the intention for your day. What does your ideal day look like? See the outcome you want. Visualize and experience it as though it has already happened. Let feelings of gratitude fill your entire being as you experience what you desire and affirm what you want with an attitude of gratitude. Speak your affirmitude out loud. Put it out to the Universe. You can re-affirmitude as often as you like. You can never overdo affirmitudes. There are no limits to the benefits you are consciously creating.

In the next chapter, I have provided a list of affirmitudes which you can use on a daily basis to increase your well-being and spiritual consciousness and ultimately improve your life. Feel free to create your own affirmitudes by affirming what you desire to feel or have and also expressing gratitude. It can change your life for the better in endless ways.

I am grateful that you have picked up this book and are reading the words on these pages. I am grateful that we are on this journey of self-betterment together. I want you to live your best life, and I am grateful that you are committed to breaking through the limiting beliefs of your past that hold you back. I am grateful that you are ready to live your best life and I dedicate this affirmitude to you:

The reader of this book is ready to live their best life. Thank you, Universe, for helping them discover and break the limited conditioning of their past. The author of this book is overflowing with divine excitement for them, and gratitude now.

17

DAILY AFFIRMITUDES

"I am connected to a higher power.
Thank you, Universe, for your
omnipotence. I am overflowing with
divine consciousness and gratitude now."
– Tania Kolar

Here is a list of daily affirmitudes which you can use any time you want to shift your emotional state, increase your consciousness, improve spiritual well-being, and/or affirm what you desire or want to feel while expressing gratitude at the same time.

Scan the alphabetical list below to determine how you are feeling or want to feel and read the corresponding affirmitude to affirm and be grateful for that which you desire.

Please feel free to substitute the word *Universe* with the word for your higher power or a word that has meaning for you.

Daily Affirmitudes

Attitude

When you can't shake your bad attitude repeat the following affirmitude:

I have a stellar attitude. Thank you, Universe, for my ever-positive outlook. I am overflowing with divine optimism and gratitude now.

Avoiding intimacy

When you feel that you are avoiding intimacy in a romantic or soulmate relationship, repeat the following affirmitude:

I am openly inviting deep love and intimacy into my relationship. Thank you, Universe, for intimate connection. I am overflowing with divine intimacy and gratitude now.

Being a role model

When you want to be a role model to guide and inspire others along their journey, repeat the following affirmitude:

I am an exemplary role model. Thank you, Universe, for allowing me to powerfully guide loved ones. I am overflowing with divine leadership and gratitude now.

Can't handle pressure

When you feel like you can't handle the pressures of work or family or society, repeat the following affirmitude:

I handle and accept any situation that comes my way. Thank you, Universe, for my innate inner strength. I am overflowing with divine power and gratitude now.

Disbelief in future

When you feel hopeless about the future, or you don't believe your present circumstances will get any better, repeat the following affirmitude:

I believe in greatness and know the best is yet to come. Thank you, Universe, for hopeful expectation. I am overflowing with divine hopefulness and gratitude now.

Discouraged

When you are feeling discouraged and disheartened repeat, the following affirmitude:

I am emboldened by the determination and confidence that surrounds me. Thank you, Universe, for eternal assistance. I am overflowing with divine encouragement and gratitude now.

Disrespected

When you feel disrespected by co-workers at your job, or by loved ones in personal relationships, repeat the following affirmitude:

I am always respected. Thank you, Universe, for the respect

I command in any given situation. I am overflowing with divine respect and gratitude now.

Emotionally spent

When you feel emotionally drained, tired, feeling like you can't do any more, repeat the following affirmitude. *I am emotionally strong. Thank you, Universe, for my emotive strength. I am overflowing with divine emotional fortitude and gratitude now.*

Enlightenment

When you are seeking a higher power and/or spiritual enlightenment repeat the following affirmitude: *I am connected to a higher power. Thank you, Universe, for your omnipotence. I am overflowing with divine consciousness and gratitude now.*

Faith

When your faith is wavering, and you doubt your belief in God, the Universe or a higher power, repeat the following affirmitude: *I feel the presence of a higher power and my faith is unbreakable. Thank you, Universe, for your magnificent presence. I am overflowing with divine reverence and gratitude now.*

Feeling afraid

When you are afraid to take risks or afraid of what might happen in the future, repeat the following affirmitude: *I am fearless, for fear is an illusion. Thank you, Universe, for my boundless courage and trust. I am overflowing with divine bravery and gratitude now.*

Feeling as if others or the Universe are conspiring against you

When you feel a sense of uncomfortableness, that others or the Universe are all conspiring against you, repeat the following affirmitude:

The Universe is on my side and brings the right people and experiences into my life at exactly the right time so that I may live to my fullest potential. Thank you, Universe, for your celestial support. I am overflowing with divine intervention and gratitude now.

Feeling defeated or wanting to give up

When you feel defeated and want to quit pursuing your goals and ideals, repeat the following affirmitude:

I am determined and unstoppable. Thank you, Universe, for my tenacity and resolve. I am overflowing with divine determination and gratitude now.

Feeling emasculated

When you feel that you are not man enough or have been emasculated, repeat the following affirmitude:

I am innately masculine. I am the epitome of masculinity. Thank you, Universe, for my manhood. I am overflowing with divine masculinity and gratitude now.

Feeling ill
When you are feeling ill repeat the following affirmitude:
I am in perfect health. Thank you, Universe, for optimal physical health. I am overflowing with divine healthiness and gratitude now.

Feeling like a failure
When you feel like a failure at anything or everything, repeat the following affirmitude.
I am a success, and everything I touch turns to gold. Thank you, Universe, for my accomplishments and gains. I am overflowing with divine achievement and gratitude now.

Feeling like there is not enough to go around for everyone
When you feel the Universe is limited and there is not enough to go around for everyone, or you believe someone else's wins have stolen your chance of abundance and opportunity, repeat the following affirmitude:
I have everything I need, and there is more than enough for everyone. Thank you, Universe, for the limitless abundance and opportunity that exists. I am overflowing with divine abundance and gratitude now.

Feeling like you have nothing to offer
When you think that you have very little or absolutely nothing to offer in a relationship, repeat the following affirmitude:
There is no one else like me. I bring unique and unlimited benefits to my partner because of my uniqueness. Thank you, Universe, for the invaluable contribution I bring to my relationship. I am overflowing with divine contribution and gratitude now.

Feeling not good enough

When you feel like you are just not good enough, will never be enough, or if you have given all you can and still feel like it's not enough, repeat the following affirmitude:

I am enough. Thank you, Universe, for my inner worth. I am overflowing with divine self-value and gratitude now.

Feeling not woman enough/less than a woman

When you feel like you are not woman enough or confused about what being a woman means anymore, repeat the following affirmitude:

I am innately feminine. I am the epitome of femininity. Thank you, Universe, for my womanhood. I am overflowing with divine femininity and gratitude now.

Feeling ordinary

When you feel ordinary, plain, boring, and not the unique, original, exciting individual you are, repeat the following affirmitude:

There is no one else on this planet that has my unique gifts. Thank you, Universe, for the individual qualities that make me extraordinary. I am overflowing with divine dynamism and gratitude now.

Feeling passionless

When you have lost passion for what you do, what you want to do or lost your inner drive, repeat the following affirmitude:

I am deeply passionate. Thank you, Universe, for igniting my inner flame. I am overflowing with divine passion and gratitude now.

Feeling stagnant

When you feel stuck in one place or are afraid to take action, repeat the following affirmitude:

I take control of my future by taking action. Thank you, Universe, for forward advancement. I am overflowing with divine action and gratitude now.

Feeling unappreciated

When you feel as though no one appreciates you or what you do for others, repeat the following affirmitude:

I am deeply appreciated. Thank you, Universe, for the validation and praise I receive. I am overflowing with divine recognition and gratitude now.

Feeling unappreciative

When you have difficulty being appreciative of others or have difficulty finding anything to be grateful for, repeat the following affirmitude:

I appreciate the wonder of the Universe. Thank you, Universe, for showing me how to appreciate both the big and little things in every day and the people who surround me. I am overflowing with divine appreciation and gratitude now.

Feeling unattractive

When you feel unattractive, ugly, that your beauty is gone, repeat the following affirmitude:

I am a beautiful divine being. Thank you, Universe, for my unique and individual beauty. I am overflowing with divine attractiveness and gratitude now.

Or

I am a handsome divine being. Thank you, Universe, for my unique good looks. I am overflowing with divine attractiveness and gratitude now.

Feeling undeserving

When you feel like you don't deserve all or any of the good that has shown up in your life, repeat the following affirmitude:

I deserve. Thank you, Universe, for my innate deservedness. I am overflowing with divine deservedness and gratitude now.

Feeling undesirable

When you feel undesired or undesirable, that no one wants you, repeat the following affirmitude:

I am desirable. Thank you, Universe, for my natural appeal. I am overflowing with divine desirability and gratitude now.

Feeling unlovable

When you feel unlovable, or you think there is no one that will love you the way you want and need to be loved, repeat the following affirmitude:

I am lovable and loved. Thank you, Universe, for the affection and adoration that surrounds me every day. I am overflowing with divine love and gratitude now.

Feeling unsafe

When you feel unsafe, uneasy, and unprotected, repeat the following affirmitude:

I am safe from harm. Thank you, Universe, for your omnipotent protection. I am overflowing with divine protection and gratitude now.

Feeling unsupported

When you feel like you have no support from those you'd want support from, repeat the following affirmitude:

I am always supported. Thank you, Universe, for unbounded support. I am overflowing with divine assistance and gratitude now.

Feeling unworthy

When you feel like you don't measure up or that you ever will measure up to other's expectations or feel unworthy of love, repeat the following affirmitude:

I was born into this world as a worthy being, and I am ready to reclaim my birth inheritance. I am whole and worthy. Thank you, Universe, for complete worthiness. I am overflowing with divine worthiness and gratitude now.

Feeling weak or disempowered

When you feel weak, feeble, or disempowered, repeat the following affirmitude:

I am strong and empowered. Thank you, Universe, for unyielding fortitude. I am overflowing with divine empowerment and gratitude now.

Feelings of poverty

When you feel impoverished, poor, barely making ends meet, repeat the following affirmitude:

I have financial security and abundance. Thank you, Universe, for unlimited monetary wealth. I am overflowing with divine wealth and gratitude now.

Forgiveness

When you find it difficult to forgive those that have hurt you or your loved ones physically, mentally or emotionally, repeat the following affirmitude:

Today, I choose to forgive and release bitterness or vengeful thoughts. Thank you, Universe, for my forgiving heart. I am overflowing with divine absolution and gratitude now.

Generosity

When you feel a lack of generosity or feel disinterested in giving, repeat the following affirmitude:

I am surrounded by generosity. Thank you, Universe, for your generosity. I am overflowing with divine philanthropy and gratitude now.

Grief/death of a loved one

When you want to heal from grief repeat the following affirmitude:

I safely process and heal my grieving heart. Thank you, Universe, for taking care of me as I process and heal my deep sorrow, pains, thoughts, and emotions. I am overflowing with divine comfort and gratitude now.

Guidance

When you feel misguided or are wanting to seek direction, repeat the following affirmitude:

I am sublimely guided by spirit. Thank you, Universe, for being a driving force and showing me the right path at the right moment. I am overflowing with divine guidance and gratitude now.

Hatefulness

When you feel hateful, or spiteful, towards others, repeat the following affirmitude:

I am kind-hearted. Thank you, Universe, for my ability to bestow kindness towards others. I am overflowing with divine benevolence and gratitude now.

Heartbreak/Loss (love)

When you feel heartbroken, repeat the following affirmitude:

I have been blessed with intimately knowing the deepest kind of love that exists. A love that lives eternally within my heart. Thank you, Universe, for showing me to the deepest love possible. I am overflowing with profound love and gratitude now.

Holding on to limiting beliefs

When it seems like you just can't let go of the limiting thoughts and beliefs from your past that keeps you from living your full potential and the extraordinary life you were meant to live, repeat the following affirmitude:

I release all limiting beliefs. Thank you, Universe, for helping me discover and break old worn-out molds of the past that no longer serve me. I am overflowing with divine certitude and gratitude now.

Honoring your gift as a healer

When you want to strengthen your healing abilities and heal others from their suffering, repeat the following affirmitude:

I am an intuitive healer. Thank you, Universe, for helping me to alleviate suffering. I am overflowing with divine healing and gratitude now.

Humanity

When you have lost faith in humanity, society, politicians, repeat the following affirmitude:

I believe in the good of all humanity. Thank you, Universe, for the inherent good that lies within each of us. I am overflowing with divine humanity and gratitude now.

Impact

When you feel you have no impact, no purpose, no reason, repeat the following affirmitude:

I powerfully affect others. Thank you, Universe, for the impression I create. I am overflowing with divine impact and gratitude now.

In need of a miracle

When you could use a miracle, wish for a miracle, or disbelieve completely in miracles repeat the following affirmitude:

I open my eyes to miracles. Thank you, Universe, for the daily miracles that surround me. I am overflowing with divine phenomenon and gratitude now.

Inability to express your emotions

When you can't freely express how you are feeling or feel like you must hide your emotions, repeat the following affirmitude:

I am safe to freely express my emotions. Thank you, Universe, for my sensitivity, empathy, and compassion. I am overflowing with divine emotion and gratitude now.

Indecision

When you are indecisive, confused, uncertain, repeat the following affirmitude:

I make good decisions in good time. Thank you, Universe, for my swift and appropriate action. I am overflowing with divine decisiveness and gratitude now.

Influence

When you feel you have no influence on others or the world, when you think your opinions don't matter, repeat the following affirmitude:

I am an effective influencer. Thank you, Universe, for the footprint I create. I am overflowing with divine influence and gratitude now.

Intelligence

When you feel you are stupid or unintelligent repeat the following affirmitude:

I am intelligent. Thank you Universe for my vast knowledge. I am overflowing with divine wisdom and gratitude now.

Joy

When you feel there is no joy in your life anymore, repeat the following affirmitude:

I radiate joy. Thank you, Universe, for the joy that fills my heart. I am overflowing with divine bliss and gratitude now.

Lack of confidence

When your confidence is low or non-existent, repeat the following affirmitude:

I am confident. Thank you, Universe, for my unwavering confidence. I am overflowing with divine assuredness and gratitude now.

Lack of prosperity

When you feel a lack of prosperity, like you don't have enough repeat the following affirmitude:

I am prosperous. Thank you Universe for good fortune and prosperity consciousness. I am overflowing with divine prosperity and gratitude now.

Low standards/poor expectations

When you have low standards and poor expectations for

yourself repeat the following affirmitude:

I set my own high standards and expect the best. Thank you, Universe, for my strong ethics and unshakeable belief. I am overflowing with divine expectation and gratitude now.

Negative thoughts

When you are consumed by constant negative thoughts and find it difficult to stay positive, repeat the following affirmitude:

I radiate positivity today. Thank you, Universe, for transmuting lower thoughts and negative energy. I am overflowing with divine optimism and gratitude now.

Nurturing

When you neglect your loved ones or don't give them the love and attention you know they deserve, repeat the following affirmitude:

I instinctively nurture others. Thank you, Universe, for allowing me to care for loved ones. I am overflowing with divine nurturing and gratitude now.

Overwhelmed

When you feel overwhelmed by responsibility, accountability or obligations, repeat the following affirmitude:

I am peaceful and calm. Thank you, Universe, for the peace and serenity of my thoughts. I am overflowing with divine tranquility and gratitude now.

Overwhelmed by clutter and chaos and disorganization

When you feel completely chaotic, out of control, or disorganized or buried by clutter, repeat the following affirmitude:

I am organized. Thank you, Universe, for my organizational abilities. I am overflowing with divine order and gratitude now.

Parenting

When you question your ability as a parent or feel overwhelmed by parenthood, repeat the following affirmitude:

I am an extraordinary mom. Thank you, Universe, for my maternal instinct. I am overflowing with divine motherly love now.

Or

I am an extraordinary dad. Thank you, Universe, for my natural paternal instinct. I am overflowing with divine fatherly love now.

Physical exhaustion

When you feel physically fatigued and lack energy, repeat the following affirmitude:

I am physically fit and strong. Thank you Universe for my sustainable stamina. I overflowing with divine endurance and gratitude now.

Purpose

When you want to live with purpose, meaning repeat the following affirmitude:

My soul is alive with profound meaning and purpose. Thank you, Universe, for definiteness of purpose. I am overflowing with divine purpose and gratitude now.

Self-hatred

When you disapprove of yourself and are directing hatred towards yourself, repeat the following affirmitude:

I love and approve of myself. Thank you, Universe, for my ability to recognize my own value and self-worth. I am overflowing with divine self-love and gratitude now.

Selfishness

When you feel selfish or feel a disinterest in giving, repeat the following affirmitude:

I give freely, generously and without attachment. Thank you, Universe, for my altruism and ability to share. I am overflowing with divine allocation and gratitude now.

Service

When you feel as though you are of no service of no use to others, repeat the following affirmitude:

I am of great service to others. Thank you, Universe, for allowing me to serve and assist others. I am overflowing with divine service and gratitude now.

Shyness

When you feel shy or introverted repeat the following affirmitude:

I am fun-loving and outgoing. Thank you, Universe, for my gregarious personality. I am overflowing with divine affability and gratitude now.

Spirituality

When you want to strengthen your spirituality, repeat the following affirmitude:

I am one with spirit. Thank you Universe for my spiritual awakening consciousness. I am overflowing with divine spirituality and gratitude now.

Talent

When you want to honor your talent, or you doubt your abilities and talents, repeat the following affirmitude:

I am intrinsically talented. Thank you, Universe, for my giftedness. I am overflowing with divine proficiency and gratitude now.

Tragedy

When you find it difficult to find the meaning in challenging times, when you are shocked at the news reports of nothing but tragic events, repeat the following affirmitude:

I find lesson and meaning in every tragedy. Thank you, Universe, for teaching me compassion and understanding so I may evolve to my fullest potential. I am overflowing with divine empathy and gratitude now.

Unhappiness

When you are experiencing feelings of unhappiness, sadness, melancholy, repeat the following affirmitude:

I choose happiness today. Thank you, Universe, for the happiness that follows me every day and everywhere I go. I am overflowing with divine contentment and gratitude now.

Unmotivated

When you lack motivation and drive, feel you have become lazy, repeat the following affirmitude:

I am highly motivated. Thank you, Universe, for my eternal zest and for propelling me into action. I am overflowing with divine action and gratitude now.

Urge to physically harm yourself

When you have the urge to physically harm or mutilate your physical body, repeat the following affirmitude:

I deeply love and care for my human body. Thank you, Universe, for this sacred temple that I am blessed to care for. I am overflowing with divine reverence and gratitude now.

18

HIGH-SPEED SPIRITUAL WI-FI – STREAMING FROM SOURCE ENERGY

"If you want to find the secrets of the Universe, think in terms of energy, frequency and vibration."
– Nikola Tesla

We've all had those magical moments in life where everything seems to be going well. You feel blissful as if the moment couldn't get any better. Everything in your life is working perfectly, and you really feel in the flow. You feel as if you are weightless or floating on air and anything and everything is possible. These are moments like finding your soul mate, the birth of a child or finding your life purpose. It feels amazing, doesn't it? The reason it feels so good is that in those moments you have tapped into a level of high vibration and consciousness. In order to get to a higher level of consciousness, you must eliminate negative thoughts and behaviors. You must get present to the now and align yourself to positive vibrations. When you raise your spiritual consciousness you will be streaming from source energy and your life will unfold in magical ways.

Your thoughts, feelings, words, actions, and beliefs all carry a vibrational frequency. Everything in the Universe has a vibration. Even the foods you eat have vibrational energy. Low-level vibrations bring low-level results. It's a barrier to living to your full potential. It is like the slow crawl of a dial-up internet connection. The signal is slow as molasses and when you finally connect it stalls, hits a dead zone and completely drops the signal and keeps you suspended in limbo. When you have reached the desired goal, and suddenly a roadblock (life challenge) pops up out of nowhere, it may be a warning you've had a drop in your spiritual connection. I'm referring to the self-created roadblocks and ones in which you have no control over.

Anxiety, worry, fear, and depression are signals that you are operating on a low vibration. When you feel you are in a low vibration, you can use that feeling as a guidepost to encourage you to change your thoughts connected to those feelings and move up to a higher vibration. Depression happens when you've lost all hope for a brighter future. This is a low-level vibration and makes it impossible to imagine a better life than you are currently living unless you increase your vibrational frequency. See beyond where you are in your current situation to get beyond it.

The first step is simply to feel a little better than you are currently feeling. You will change your vibration little by little. Try moving your body, going for a walk or doing some form of physical activity. Physical exercise releases positive endorphins which are known as the body's natural feel-good chemicals. Use movement as a way to break your pattern, change your state of mind and feel better. Chronic depression can be debilitating without proper medical attention. However, cognitive behavioral psychotherapy has been proven effective with or without medication. This type of treatment addresses patterns of thinking. Shifting your thinking to higher-level thoughts is beneficial. When you switch your thoughts to a positive vibration, you are immediately tapping into a stronger signal and are resonating at a higher frequency level. This is a universal source energy where everything originated from and where limitless abundance exists. When you operate from this universal source energy all areas of your life will improve, and you are assured of a direct connection to your best self.

When you watch a video with a low connection, the video will take a long time to stream, or it will keep pausing until it can connect to a stronger signal. When things aren't going well, or nothing seems to be progressing in your life, it's like entering a wireless dead zone. All your desires, rewards, blessings, health, happiness and wealth are suspended in the dead zone waiting to be released when you can reconnect to high-speed spiritual Wi-Fi.

When there are other networks sharing your connection

your signal may be weak and slow. That is a sign you are not living *on purpose* or when you are influenced by the opinion of others. In order to stay connected to a higher vibration, you must avoid negative energy of all kinds, including the things you say, do, and feel and the people you spend time with. Being *on purpose* is like having a strong and secure high-speed connection.

When you resonate at high-speed spiritual Wi-Fi, you are connecting to the unlimited abundance available to you. You can tap into the appropriate frequency by shifting your thoughts, but you have to want to change your thoughts. Negative experiences can be difficult to get through but if you are willing, start with the desire to shift low-level vibrations. This includes thoughts, feelings, beliefs, and negative memories. The shift to a higher vibration can come as quickly as simply wanting to change your thoughts. Any resistance you are feeling is attached to a lesser vibration. You can't move to a higher vibration if you choose to hold onto lower vibrational energies.

The Universe is collaborating for your greater good. It's working for you not against you. When you take on this viewpoint, you can move forward with blind faith knowing there is a definitive purpose to all experiences. Even when things are not working in your favor, you will begin to see that even low vibrations serve a purpose in your life. According to Apple founder Steve Jobs "You can't connect the dots looking forward; you can only connect them looking backward. So you have to trust that the dots will somehow connect in your future. You have to trust in something- your gut, destiny, life, karma, whatever". The dots or life experiences, have led you to exactly the right place and exactly where you need to be right now. Trust that there is a purpose or lesson behind all your experiences, even the bad ones. I urge you to let go of low-level thinking so you can move to a higher vibration and start streaming from source energy. Be inquisitive by examining negative thought patterns. Make a decision to transcend the lower vibrations that keep you tethered to a slow dial-up connection. Move beyond negativity and self-sabotaging behaviors and tap into unlimited high-speed spiritual Wi-Fi and start streaming from source energy.

When you gossip or judge others, you are operating from a low-frequency level. You feel low vibrations in the form of feeling uneasiness, feeling drained or a heaviness. Contrast that feeling with how you feel when you are in love. When you are in love you feel weightlessness, you feel energized and at ease because love is a high vibration. You can consciously tune in to your frequency and practice shifting from low vibrations. Think of someone or something you dislike. Now, think of someone or something you love. Imagine they are standing right in front of you. See them smiling back at you and notice how that feels to you. Can you feel the contrast between the two? You can recreate this feeling throughout your day any time you want to shift your vibration from low-frequency to a higher vibration.

I believe some things in life that are beyond our control are destined by fate or karma and meant to serve our greater good and ultimately a higher purpose. There may be nothing in your control that could prevent that which is fated to happen; however, you can always raise your vibrational frequency and stream from source energy. There were a series of odd or coincidental happenings that occurred surrounding my assault which has led me to believe that this event was destined to happen.

Firstly, the name of the woman who was strangled and murdered in an underground parking lot, years before, kept running through my mind for an entire week before I was assaulted. I had no personal connection to her and couldn't understand why I would be thinking about her. Next, I had a feeling I couldn't shake that something bad was going to happen, I felt like it was a sign to prepare and brace myself for what was to come. Then, the friend whose house I was at for dinner normally would have been working that evening and was given the night off last minute. Next, my attacker would not have been able to get into the underground parking behind me had a car not exited shortly after I entered. Also, if I hadn't held the entrance door open for a few seconds, I would have been able to close the door on my attacker. Also, in a bizarre twist, the suspect called Crime Stoppers and blamed his neighbor, an ex-friend, so he could collect the reward. That call indirectly led police to him instead.

Additionally, when I was asked to see if I could identify my attacker through a set of photos, I quickly dismissed them as not being him. However, I paused at one picture for a few seconds because there was something kind of similar to the man who attacked me, but I knew it wasn't him. The photo I paused on was the ex-friend. He was considered a primary suspect because of the Crime Stoppers lead, so police believed they found the perpetrator. If I didn't pause on the photo, they probably wouldn't have sent a swat police team to apprehend the wrong person. Lastly, ironically, the attacker was home when the swat team swarmed his townhouse complex to arrest his neighbor, and he mistakenly believed they were coming to arrest him. He tried to kill himself and was taken to the hospital. When he was asked why he tried to kill himself, he confessed that he was responsible for the attack. Given the odd or coincidental happenings, I believe what had happened to me was meant to happen as part of my life's purpose. Nonetheless, I had to work really hard to avoid getting stuck in low vibrational energies.

Over time, you can slowly inch your way out of low-level energies and overcome negative thoughts and limiting beliefs. You may have no control over the circumstances that present, but you can always raise your vibrational frequency and stream from source energy. Remember, when you are experiencing low vibrational energy change your thoughts and get up and move your body. Go for a walk, dance, phone a friend or clean the house. In tough times shift your vibration little by little. You will change your vibration no matter how small the action is. Make the switch from a low vibration slow speed connection and upgrade to high-speed spiritual

Wi-Fi and stream from source energy. The happiness, prosperity, and abundance that is destined to be yours by birth will be unleashed with lightning speed.

19

AN ABUNDANT UNIVERSE WHERE THERE IS MORE THAN ENOUGH

"I am one with the Power that created me. I am totally open and receptive to the abundant flow of prosperity that the Universe offers. All my needs and desires are met before I even ask. I am Divinely guided and protected, and I make choices that are beneficial for me. I rejoice in other's successes, knowing there is plenty for us all."

– Louise Hay

Do you ever feel like someone is trying to take what is yours or you can't have what you want because someone already has it? There is no need to panic as there is more than enough to go around for everyone. The Universe is abundant and limitless. This is clearly evidenced in nature. Just take a look at the endless expanse of blue sky or the plants and trees in a forest nourished by the abundance of air, sunlight, and soil. There is a natural abundance available to you. When you are open to abundance, you will begin to see it show up everywhere and will be able to receive what the Universe wants to give you.

You have the ability to manifest absolutely anything that you desire through the power of your thoughts and imagination. You can create into existence that which you desire by imaging what it is that you want. See it in your mind and believe it has already shown up for you and you will materialize it into being. What you desire may not show up in the exact way you expect it. You must let go of any expectations of how things are supposed to happen in your life. It's the job of the Universe to figure out how your desire will show up. Your job is to be open and willing to receive it when it does show up for you. If it's a romantic relationship you want, don't discard the ideal man that shows up just because he is not your usual type or for something trivial like the wrong hair color. When you are fixated on a pre-conceived notion on how what you want must show up, you may actually miss it when it appears because you were too pre-occupied expecting something else. What is actually there for you becomes unnoticeable and therefore unavailable to you.

Although you may be following your intuition and putting in the work to manifest what you want, you may still feel like your desires are out of reach. If you haven't seen any results, you may be tempted to give up. It's like the Amaryllis bulb I planted. I soaked the bulb for hours before I planted it. I got an appropriate pot and pressed the soil to secure it firmly into place. I watered it as necessary, and there seemed to be no growth for weeks.

I thought my Amaryllis was never going to bloom. One day I could see it open a tiny bit. But again, the next day it seemed to not move at all. Surprisingly, a few days later it had three full exotic blooms and another one on the way. I couldn't believe how quickly it bloomed after taking so long to see any growth at all. It was a vibrant, flourishing plant that I almost gave up on. Like the amaryllis bulb, even though you may not see any results at the moment, things can blossom for you when you least expect it. Don't give up on your goals and the things you want to manifest in your life because you are closer than you think.

The Universe is resourceful and will find ways to bring you what you truly desire. Albeit unconventional at times. A new pair of shiny grey heels showed up in front of my mother's condo. Her desire allowed her to manifest the shoes. She had an uncommon shoe size because of her tiny feet. The shoes looked brand new and unworn. They were sitting there in front of the building as if waiting for her to step into them. They were the perfect fit for her. Be aware of what shows up and make sure to be able to receive what you've asked for. If you create reasons why you can't have what you want you are blocking it from being manifested into existence. Let go of controlling how it will show up. Just be willing to accept it when it does show up.

Today, I get great satisfaction from putting new or slightly used items that I don't use in a bag, and I put it near the entrance to where I live. I will add a little note saying: *Free to a good home, I'm new, I still work, Just for you*, or simply *Enjoy!* The items are usually gone within a couple of hours. I think of my mom and how happy she was to receive her shiny new grey shoes and I hope I've made someone just as happy, by helping manifest something they desired.

Do you ever notice that when you really want something, somehow it shows up? Or do you ever get a strong inner urge to do something or take action? Those urges are nudges from the Universe. Don't ignore the urge or nudge to take action because it didn't come at a convenient time or show up as you intended. When you come up with excuses and don't follow through on the intuitive guidance, you may be blocking that which you want to be manifested from entering into your life. For example, let's say you want to manifest a loving, committed relationship. For the next few weeks, you are constantly noticing flyers or receiving brochures for dance lessons in your area. Then, coincidentally your friend mentions she wants to take dance lessons and asks you to join her. You listen to your intuition and agree to sign up. On the day of the lessons, you don't feel like going because you're too tired. You feel a nudge to go, so you end up going anyway. You have a great time, and you meet the man of your dreams, and he asks you out. If you ignored the intuitive guidance you might miss out on meeting your future partner at an event you didn't attend.

I was on a flight heading home to Toronto from the U.S. I hadn't realized, until I was on the plane that the airline implemented a new policy and no longer accepted cash on board. I wanted to order a glass of wine but I knew my credit card was maxed out, so, when the snack and beverage cart came along, I had no choice but to pass. I sat in my seat wishing I had a glass of wine to enjoy. Several minutes into the flight the steward leaned in beside me and said "I would like to bring you a glass of wine." I wanted to accept his offer but instead said…"thank you so much, but I'm good thanks" and turned down the free drink. My refusal prompted an onboard self-analysis. I sat there for the rest of the flight wondering why I refused the gift of a glass of wine that I wanted. Why was I making it difficult for me to get what I wanted? Did I feel I didn't deserve to get what I wanted? Was I afraid of being judged? Would the steward know my credit card was maxed out and think I was overspending? I have no idea why the steward offered to bring me a glass of wine other than the fact I manifested it. I clearly lacked the willingness to accept the gift. I was standing in my own way and blocking what the Universe was trying to give me. The glass of wine is symbolic for anything you desire. What are you blocking or saying no to? Accept the complimentary glass of wine for goodness sakes. Your gifts are waiting. The Universe is your benevolent benefactor.

If you are having a hard time manifesting what you want you can repeat the following affirmitude:

I am a master at manifesting. Thank you Universe, I am grateful for the abundance and limitless gifts that show up in my life on a daily basis because of my belief and acceptance. Thank you Universe I am overflowing with divine manifestation and gratitude now.

From as young as I can remember, I wanted to be an actor. When I was about thirteen years old, I decided I was too old. I know it seems ridiculous now, but at the time the belief was very real to me. There was a girl in my elementary school who landed a recurring role in a TV series. I felt defeated because I felt my career was over. Someone I knew was already doing what I wanted to do. I had a belief that there was not enough to go around for me. I believed because this girl was given an acting opportunity, there was no room left for me. I squashed my passion because I didn't believe it was possible for me.

A few years later, I took a job waitressing at a hotel. The only reason I took the job was that the hotel also had a dinner theatre. I ended up working there for a few years. In all that time, I never told a single person I wanted to be an actor. I was too afraid of failure and not being good enough. If I never told anyone I wanted to be on stage, then no one would know I wasn't good enough. Fear prevented me from expressing my desires. I continued to deny my desire for many years until I could no longer stand the feeling of regret. I started researching how to get into the acting business. I found a bookstore, I never knew existed, that only sold books related to the acting industry. Just being in the bookstore was a huge step for me. Something just felt right. I was doing something for me. I was literally shaking as I purchased the stack of books and videos that were piled in my arms. The feeling of being authentic and on the right path was palpable. My entire body was shaking in anticipation of the good that was ahead of me.

On my drive home I broke down in tears. I'm talking about a thirty-year-flood of pent-up-tears-kind-of-cry. I cried tears of grief, sadness, repression, relief, and happiness. I couldn't stop the tears from flowing. For the first time in decades, I didn't try to squash what I was feeling. I didn't care who saw me cry. I was oblivious to all the cars and people around me. It felt incredible to release decades of stored emotion. Something changed inside me that day. I felt lighter, exhilarated and reignited with passion. It all started with the decision to do something for myself that was important to me. At that moment, I changed my belief that there was not enough to go around for me. I understood that the Universe is limitless and that it was me holding myself back.

You can reclaim lost desires and allow abundance to flow into your life. Don't take yourself out of the game of life because you believe someone else already has what you want. Be authentic and reclaim the lost desires and the limitless universal abundance that always was yours and always will be yours for the taking.

The Natural Balance of Giving and Receiving

One of life's universal laws is the Law of Giving and Receiving. This dynamic exchange is witnessed in everything from the air we breathe in and out, a compliment or the monetary payout we receive for a job or service we have given and is evidenced in nature.

"And now you ask in your heart, 'How shall we distinguish that which is good in pleasure from that which is not good?' Go to your fields and your gardens, and you shall learn that it is the pleasure of the bee to gather honey of the flower, But it is also the pleasure of the flower to yield its honey to the bee. For to the bee a flower is a fountain of life, and to the flower a bee is a messenger of love, And to both, bee and flower, the giving and the receiving of pleasure is a need and an ecstasy. People of Orphalese, be in your pleasures like the flowers and the bees."
– Khalil Gibran, The Prophet

Like the bee to the flower, and the flower to the bee there is a natural balance of giving and receiving. Be mindful that you are not throwing off the balance of giving and receiving in your life. My dad was slicing a peach and asked if I would like a piece. It looked juicy and delicious, and I wanted a piece but said I didn't. I sensed his disappointment when I declined. I realized, my seemingly selfless act was blocking the gift my father was trying to give me. So instead, I told my father I changed my mind and would love a piece. In declining, I believed I was leaving more fruit for my dad to enjoy. It was simple, I wanted a piece of fruit, and my dad wanted to give it to me. It was a classic example of the natural flow of the Law of Giving and Receiving. However, I stopped the flow until I changed my mind.

If you go to a restaurant and always fight to pay the bill, then you are not allowing others the enjoyment of treating you. I am not saying that you should always let someone else pick up the bill, but you should at least once in a while in the spirit of giving and receiving. The Universe thrives on giving and receiving so don't forget to pay it forward. When you always refuse a glass of wine, a piece of fruit, an offer to pay or a gift, then you are throwing off the equilibrium of give and take. The key is finding the right balance. The Universe is abundant. There is no need to sacrifice your desires for the sake of others. Constantly putting others needs before your own is also throwing off the balance of the Law of Giving and Receiving.

Another example is staying in a relationship when you don't love your partner. You make a decision to stay because your partner will be happy even though you will be miserable. You put their needs above your own and believe you are doing them a favor when in fact you're hurting them and you. You may feel temporarily appeased because you're avoiding the pain of a breakup and sparing your partner's feelings, but this can only be temporary given the situation.

You are depriving your partner of the opportunity to be loved in the way he or she deserves to be loved. Ultimately, what you are doing by staying in a relationship, that is not right for you, is postponing your partner's happiness and also your own. You each deserve an authentic relationship aligned with a healthy balance of giving and receiving. Get present to the dynamic exchange of giving and receiving and make sure that you are not blocking one or the other. How you accept or reject the small things in life, like a piece of fruit, is also how you accept or reject the big things.

When you only give you miss the joy of receiving. When you only receive you miss the joy of giving. Like inhaling and exhaling one cannot exist without the other. You cannot take a breath in without letting a breath out. There is a natural and effortless balance of giving and receiving, and benefit to both the giver and the receiver.

20

LIVING AN EXTRAORDINARY LIFE OF GREATNESS

"The greater danger for most of us lies not in setting our aim too high and falling short; but in setting our aim too low, and achieving our mark."
— Michelangelo

What does it mean to live a life of greatness? The definition of greatness is different for everyone depending upon your wants and desires, but the essence of living a life of greatness is to live the life of your dreams without any limitations. Live with passion, and do what makes you truly happy and ignites your inner flame. There are no limitations to what you can have, what you can be, and what you can accomplish. Even if you are unsure of what you want, you can live a life of greatness by deciding to be better than you are right now and working towards attaining that goal. Set goals you think are impossible and work to obtain them anyway. Wherever you direct your focus is where your journey will lead you. So choose to live an extraordinary life of greatness.

I want you to live a remarkable life. Live largely and dare to be your best self. This is who you were meant to be. Shine your inner light like the golden Buddha. Be accountable for your future and make your life extraordinary. Take action to edge past your fear and step out of your comfort zone. A major life overhaul is only a thought away. Breathe into the extraordinary life that is already yours. Make it your mission to stop the self-sabotage and limiting beliefs of your past. Now is your time to radiate your truth, your beautiful and authentic self and allow a remarkable life to unfold.

When you believe there are no limitations you can achieve anything. Set high goals and be committed to the pursuit of them. Remember, you were born to live a life of greatness. Step out of the limitations of your past and enter into the space of greatness where anything is possible. Doing the work to uncover and break your stupid mold, coupled with understanding the lessons in all of your challenges, and experiences are the roadmap to your best self.

Celebrate the magnificence of your authentic self and live a life of greatness that was destined to be yours by virtue of being born into this extraordinary world as your extraordinary self. You are remarkable and deserve living an extraordinary life. By using the techniques outlined in this book, you will break your stupid mold, and overcome the limitations of your past and step into a new life. An extraordinary life of greatness is waiting for you. Go get it! You've got this!

ABOUT THE AUTHOR

Tania Kolar is a motivational speaker, international TV personality, online radio host, and life coach. After suffering a traumatic personal tragedy, with only her determination and sheer willpower, Tania was able to overcome the anguish and deep emotional pain. She feels strongly that what she learned and how she was able to heal is now her life's mission to share, and to help others do the same. Tania is passionate about empowering and inspiring change that will create lasting transformation in people's lives. She believes it's a journey and it just takes one step to start.

To find out more about Tania Kolar please visit: www.taniakolar.com